LONDON
LANDMARKS

getmapping® + HarperCollins*Publishers*

LONDON LANDMARKS

AMAZING VIEWS FROM
www.getmapping.com

First published in 2002 by
HarperCollinsPublishers
77–85 Fulham Palace Road
London W6 8JB

The HarperCollins website address is:
www.fireandwater.com

Photography © 2002 Getmapping plc

Getmapping plc hereby asserts its moral right to be identified as the author
of this work.

Getmapping can produce an individual print of any area shown in this book,
or of any area within the United Kingdom. The image can be centred
wherever you choose, printed at any size from A6 to 7.5 metres square, and
at any scale up to 1:1,000. For further information, please contact
Getmapping on 0845 0551550, or log on to www.getmapping.com

The publisher regrets that it can accept no responsibility for any errors or
omissions within this publication, or for any expense of loss thereby caused.

A CIP catalogue record for this book is available from the British Library.

ISBN: 0 00 714416 4

Text by Ian Harrison
Design by Colin Brown
Photographic image processing by Getmapping plc
Colour origination by Colourscan, Singapore
Printed and bound by Editoriale Johnson SpA, Bergamo, Italy

contents

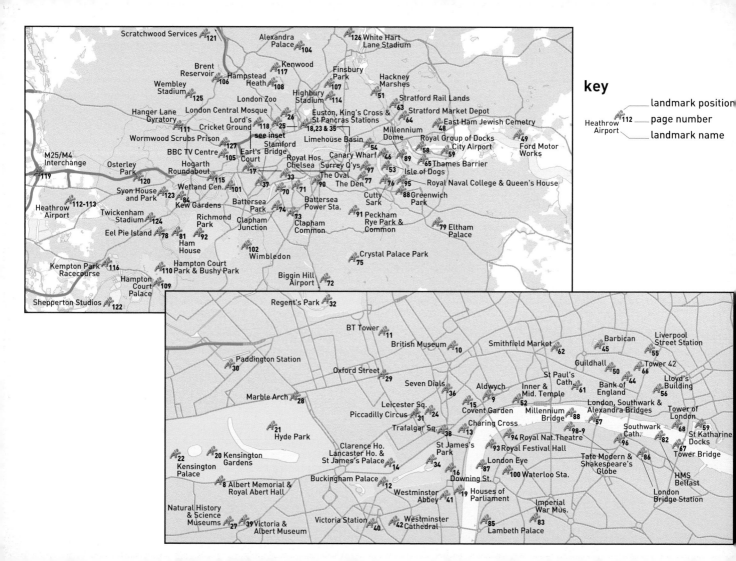

west end and central london

Albert Memorial and Royal Albert Hall
Knightsbridge, SW7

1. Date built: 1867-71 (Hall)/1876 (Memorial)
2. Architects: HY Darracott Scott (Hall)/George Gilbert Scott (Memorial)
3. Hall founded by: Sir Henry Cole
4. Dimensions: Hall 272 ft by 238 ft oval, 135 ft high/Memorial 180 ft high
5. Historic events: The "Proms" moved to the Royal Albert Hall in 1941 after the bombing of Queen's Hall

London Photographic Atlas: Page 66

Tel: (020) 7589 3203
www.royalalberthall.com

Part of Prince Albert's dream for the furtherance of art and science following the Great Exhibition was the establishment of a central hall of libraries, lecture theatres and exhibition rooms. Ironically, it was Albert's own memorial that almost destroyed that dream – the memorial fund barely covered the cost of Scott's elaborate designs for what is now the Albert Memorial, and plans for the hall were abandoned. Two years later Sir Henry Cole revived the idea, financed by a 999-year leasehold of seats that still holds good today. When Queen Victoria laid the foundation stone of the new hall she unexpectedly announced that instead of its intended title of the Central Hall of Arts and Sciences, the building was to be called the Royal Albert Hall of Arts and Sciences.

Aldwych
Strand, WC2

1. Date opened: 1905
2. Architect: London County Council
3. Origin of name: Anglo-Saxon Aldwic, meaning old settlement
4. Buildings: St Mary-le-Strand, Bush House, Australia House, India House
5. Historic events: Dickens's parents married at St Mary-le-Strand (1809)

London Photographic Atlas: Page 59

The distinctive "D" of Aldwych forms the crescent link between the Strand and Kingsway. It was conceived as part of the last great Victorian metropolitan improvement scheme, although it was Victoria's successor who officiated at the opening ceremony – in 1905 Edward VII declared the development open, and Kingsway was named in his honour.

British Museum
Bloomsbury, WC1

1. Date founded: 1753 (opened to the public 1759)
2. Architect: Robert Smirke
3. Founded by: Act of Parliament to purchase Sloane and Harleian Collections
4. Artefacts: Elgin marbles, Roman and Greek art, Egyptian collection
5. Features: The Round Reading Room (Sydney Smirke, 1852-57), the Great Court (enclosed by Sir Norman Foster, 2000)

London Photographic Atlas: Page 46

Tel: (020) 7636 1555
www.thebritishmuseum.ac.uk

The origins of the British Museum lie with Sir Hans Sloane, the Chelsea doctor after whom Sloane Square is named. During his lifetime, Sloane amassed a collection of over 80,000 curios which he bequeathed to George II for £20,000. The king declined the offer, so Parliament bought the collection and set up a foundation to house it, resulting in the world's first public museum. The BM is now one of Britain's most popular tourist attractions, with more than six million visitors each year.

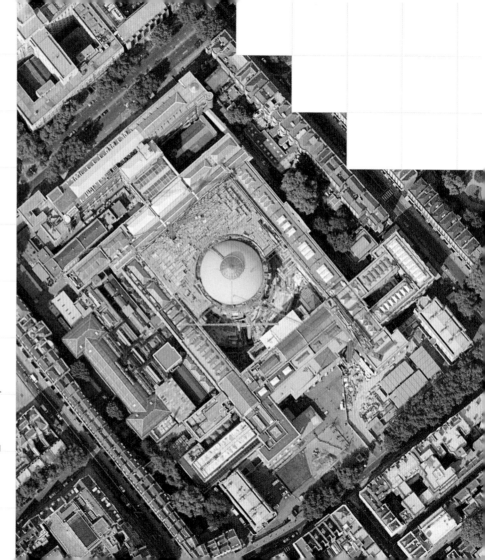

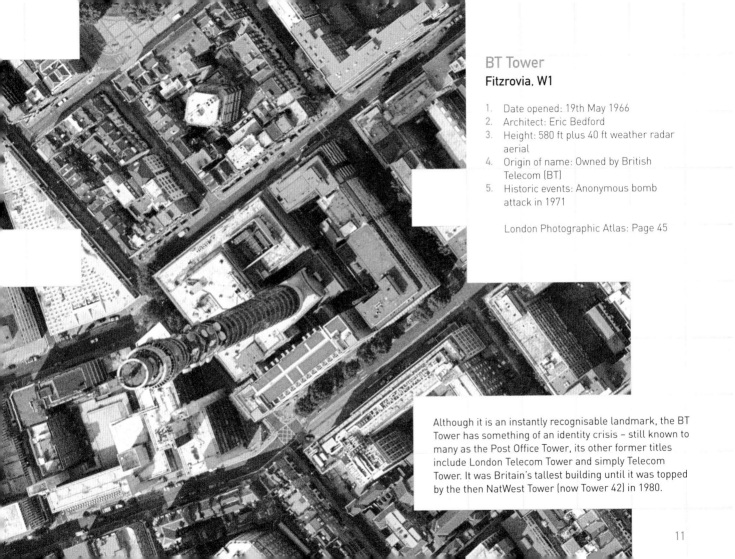

BT Tower
Fitzrovia, W1

1. Date opened: 19th May 1966
2. Architect: Eric Bedford
3. Height: 580 ft plus 40 ft weather radar aerial
4. Origin of name: Owned by British Telecom (BT)
5. Historic events: Anonymous bomb attack in 1971

London Photographic Atlas: Page 45

Although it is an instantly recognisable landmark, the BT Tower has something of an identity crisis – still known to many as the Post Office Tower, its other former titles include London Telecom Tower and simply Telecom Tower. It was Britain's tallest building until it was topped by the then NatWest Tower (now Tower 42) in 1980.

Buckingham Palace
St James's, SW1

1. Date built: 1702-5/1820-37
2. Architects: William Winde/John Nash/ Edward Blore
3. Origin of name: Originally built for 1st Duke of Buckingham and Normanby
4. Family connection: Buckingham/Crown
5. Historic events: Bombed nine times during WWII

London Photographic Atlas: Page 69

Tel: (020) 7839 1377
www.royal.gov.uk

Buckingham Palace has been the monarch's official residence for a surprisingly short time – only since 1837, when Queen Victoria moved in. The palace was designed as a three-sided open court with Marble Arch providing a grand entrance, but the courtyard was later enclosed by the familiar east façade, while Marble Arch was moved to its present position at the end of Oxford Street.

Charing Cross Station and Embankment Place
Charing Cross, WC2

1. Date opened: 1864 (rebuilt 1905/1999)
2. Architect: John Hawkshaw (hotel by EM Barry)/Terry Farrell
3. Origin of name: Close to the site of a cross erected at Charing, meaning bend (in the river)
4. Built for: South Eastern Railway Company
5. Features: Replica of the original Charing Cross

London Photographic Atlas: Page 59

Sir John Betjeman considered the dining room of the seven-storey Charing Cross Hotel, which forms the station façade, to be the most finely appointed in London". The single-arch roof of Hawkshaw's trainshed was also celebrated for its architecture but collapsed during maintenance in 1905, killing six men and destroying the Avenue Theatre next door, which has since been rebuilt as The Playhouse. The replacement roof was later demolished to make way for Embankment Place, Terry Farrell's spectacular office complex built above the station.

13

Clarence House, Lancaster House and St James's Palace
St James's, SW1

1. Date built: 1828 (CH)/1825-41 (LH)/1532 (StJ's)
2. Architects: John Nash (CH)/Benjamin Dean Wyatt (LH)/for Henry VIII (StJ's)
3. Origin of name: Built for William, Duke of Clarence (later William IV) (CH)/Named after the native county of one-time owner Viscount Leverhulme (LH)/Built on the site of St James's in the Fields (StJ's)
4. Family connection: Crown (CH)/Crown, Stafford, Dukes of Sutherland, Leverhulme, government (LH)/Crown (StJ's)
5. Historic events: Used as HQ of Red Cross and St John's Ambulance Brigade (CH, WWII)/Used for Coronation Banquet (LH, 1953)/Marriage of Queen Victoria & Prince Albert (StJ's, 1840)

London Photographic Atlas: Page 57

When the Duke of Clarence ascended the throne, a passageway was built connecting Clarence House with St James's Palace so that he could continue living in the house Nash had built for him. Clarence House was the home of the Queen Mother from 1953 until her death in 2002. Lancaster House is used for government receptions and conferences, most famously the Lancaster House Conferences deciding the futures of Kenya (1960, 62 & 63) and Rhodesia – now Zimbabwe – (1979). St James's Palace was built in the 16th century, but did not become the official residence of the monarch until the reign of William III.

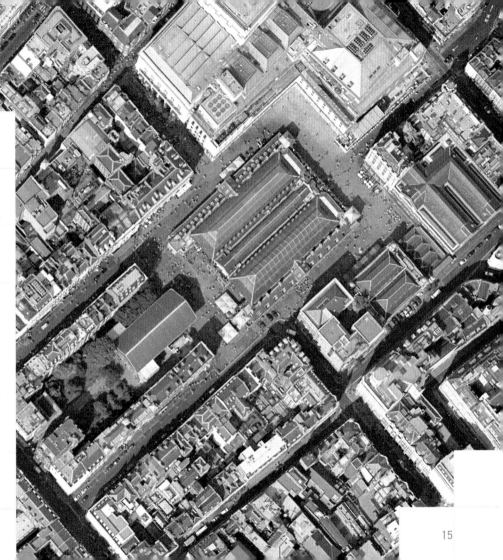

Covent Garden
Covent Garden, WC2

1. Date piazza laid out: 1627-39
2. Architect: Inigo Jones
3. Origin of name: Once a garden belonging to a convent (Long Acre was a long, narrow acre of market gardens)
4. Buildings: Royal Opera House, Apple Market, Jubilee Market, St Paul's Church
5. Historic events: Covent Garden Market moved to Nine Elms in 1974, having been held here since 1656

London Photographic Atlas: Page 59

After the Dissolution of the Monasteries this land was given to the 1st Earl of Bedford. The 4th Earl had the piazza laid out in the style of the Piazza d'Arme in Livorno, Italy, and built luxury houses "fitt for the habitacions of Gentlemen" but in 1670 the 5th Earl was granted a royal charter to hold a market at Covent Garden, reversing the 4th Earl's attempts at gentrification. The famous fruit and vegetable market finally moved to Nine Elms in 1974 and the area was earmarked for development into office blocks. Fortunately these plans were never realized and Covent Garden is now a thriving area of trendy shops, pavement cafés, bars and restaurants. To the north-west of the piazza is the Royal Opera House, which was redeveloped at the turn of the millennium.

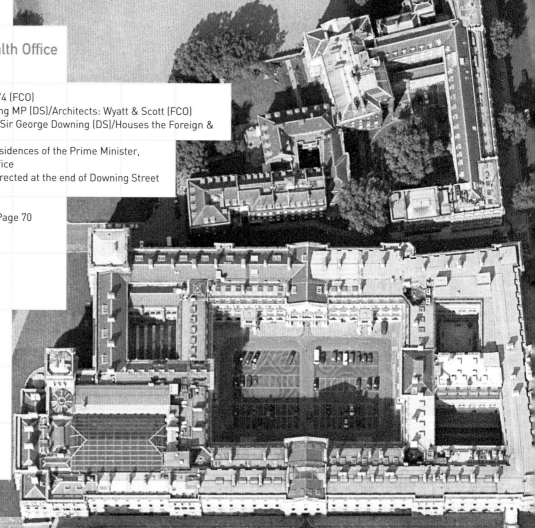

Downing Street and Foreign & Commonwealth Office
Whitehall, SW1

1. Date built: c1680 (DS)/1861–74 (FCO)
2. Developer: Sir George Downing MP (DS)/Architects: Wyatt & Scott (FCO)
3. Origin of name: Named after Sir George Downing (DS)/Houses the Foreign & Commonwealth Office (FCO)
4. Buildings: Nos 10,11 & 12, residences of the Prime Minister, Chancellor & Party Whips' office
5. Historic events: Gates were erected at the end of Downing Street in 1990 for security reasons

London Photographic Atlas: Page 70

Tel: (020) 7270 1500 (FCO)

George Downing built fifteen houses on Downing Street, of which just three survive. Some became government offices in 1694, and No. 10 became the Treasury Office. George II offered a large house backing on to No. 10 as a gift to Sir Robert Walpole, but Walpole would only accept it in his official capacity. Since then No. 10, including the L-shaped annexe, has been the official residence of the Prime Minister – a post still officially known as First Lord of the Treasury.

Earl's Court Exhibition Centre
Earl's Court, SW5

1. Date opened: 1937 (EC1)/1991 (EC2)
2. Architect: C Howard Crane (EC1)/RMJM Architects (EC2)
3. Origin of name: The courthouse of the Earls of Warwick and Holland
4. Exhibition space: 50,000 sq. yards (EC1)/20,330 sq. yards (EC2)
5. Exhibitions: Royal Smithfield Show, London International Boat Show, International Food Exhibition, Ideal Home Exhibition, London Motor Show

London Photographic Atlas: Page 76

Tel: (020) 7385 1200
www.eco.co.uk

Entertainment at Earl's Court goes back to 1887, when the Earl's Court pleasure ground was opened by JR Whitely on the derelict land between the railway lines – attractions included the Great wheel and Buffalo Bill's Wild West Show. The pleasure ground closed in 1914 and after the First World War the Empress Hall was built where the tri-concave Empress State Building now stands. In 1937 the Earl's Court Exhibition Hall (now Earl's Court One) opened with an exhibition of confectionery and chocolate, and it is now Europe's largest indoor arena, with a capacity of 20,000. In 1991 Diana, Princess of Wales, opened Earl's Court Two, whose 82-foot high arched roof echoes the architecture of the original Empress Hall.

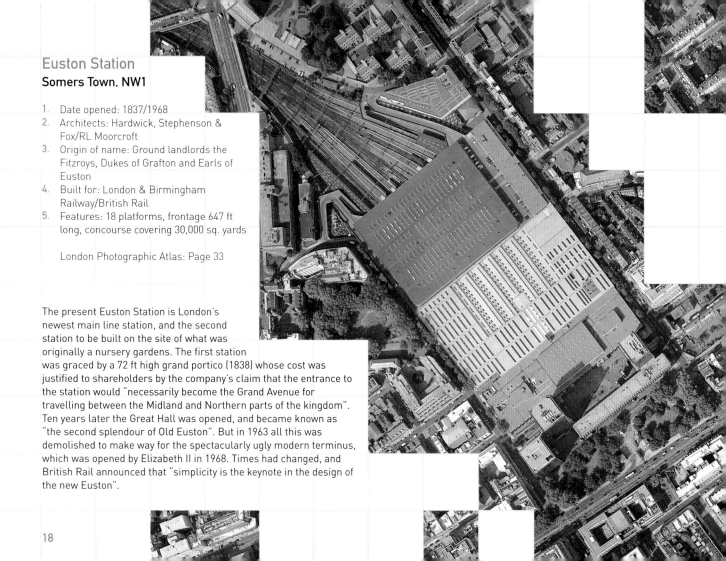

Euston Station
Somers Town, NW1

1. Date opened: 1837/1968
2. Architects: Hardwick, Stephenson & Fox/RL Moorcroft
3. Origin of name: Ground landlords the Fitzroys, Dukes of Grafton and Earls of Euston
4. Built for: London & Birmingham Railway/British Rail
5. Features: 18 platforms, frontage 647 ft long, concourse covering 30,000 sq. yards

London Photographic Atlas: Page 33

The present Euston Station is London's newest main line station, and the second station to be built on the site of what was originally a nursery gardens. The first station was graced by a 72 ft high grand portico (1838) whose cost was justified to shareholders by the company's claim that the entrance to the station would "necessarily become the Grand Avenue for travelling between the Midland and Northern parts of the kingdom". Ten years later the Great Hall was opened, and became known as "the second splendour of Old Euston". But in 1963 all this was demolished to make way for the spectacularly ugly modern terminus, which was opened by Elizabeth II in 1968. Times had changed, and British Rail announced that "simplicity is the keynote in the design of the new Euston".

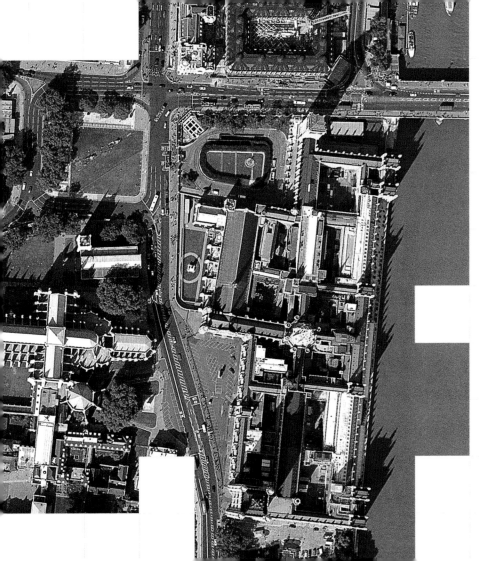

Houses of Parliament (Palace of Westminster)
Westminster, SW1

1. Date built: 1097/1834–52
2. Architects: (Built for) William Rufus/(rebuilt by) Sir Charles Barry
3. Origin of name: Site of a 10th-century minster built on Thorney Island to the west of the City of London
4. Function: Royal palace, now the Houses of Parliament
5. Historic events: Destroyed by fire 1834, bombed eleven times during WWII

London Photographic Atlas: Page 70

The Houses of Parliament are officially known as the Palace of Westminster. The first palace here was built by King Canute, and the Palace of Westminster remained the official residence of the reigning monarch and his court until it was abandoned by Henry VIII in 1532. After this parliament continued to meet at Westminster, so that for the first time the monarch's residence and the administrative centre of the kingdom were separated. On 16th October 1834 the palace burned to the ground and was rebuilt around the surviving Westminster Hall (1097) as a purpose-built home for both Houses of Parliament. The Clock Tower, popularly known as Big Ben, has become a symbol of democracy and one of London's best-loved landmarks.

Kensington Gardens
Kensington/Bayswater, W2

1. Date opened to the public: c. 1727
2. Laid out by: Wise, Bridgman, Kent, Queen Caroline
3. Area: 275 acres
4. Features: Round Pond, Diana Princess of Wales Memorial Playground
5. Historic events: George II was robbed of "his money, his watch and the buckles on his shoes" (c. 1730)

London Photographic Atlas: Page 53

Kensington Gardens were once the private gardens of Kensington Palace, and were first opened to the public by George II and Queen Caroline, although only on Sundays and only to "respectably dressed people". Queen Caroline took a great interest in the gardens, working with William Kent to create the Round Pond in 1728, and in 1730 damming the Westbourne River and joining together its marshy ponds to create the Serpentine. The bulk of the Serpentine lies in Hyde Park, and the part of it that extends into Kensington Gardens is officially known as the Long Water, despite the fact that both are part of the same body of water – similarly Hyde Park and Kensington Gardens are officially separate although it is difficult to notice the transition when walking from one to the other.

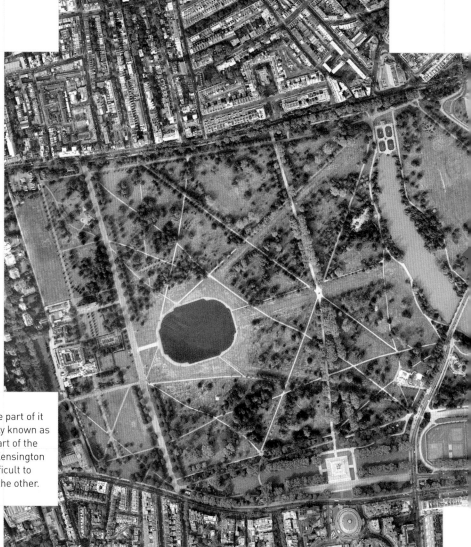

Hyde Park

Mayfair, Bayswater, Belgravia & Knightsbridge, W1, W2, SW1 & SW7

1. Date created: c. 1536 (opened to the public 17th century)
2. Created for: Henry VIII (opened to the public by James I)
3. Origin of name: The Saxon word for 100 acres, although the park is now much bigger than that
4. Area: 341 acres
5. Features: The Serpentine, Rotten Row, Speaker's Corner

London Photographic Atlas: Page 54

Tel: (020) 7298 2100
www.royalparks.gov.uk

Hyde Park was seized from the church by Henry VIII, opened to the public by James I, enclosed with a brick wall by Charles II, and had a private road built across it by William III. This road was aptly known as the Route du Roi, or King's Road, a name since corrupted to Rotten Row. At the time the road was built Hyde Park was notorious for highwaymen (one was hanged in 1687 for killing a woman who had swallowed her wedding ring to prevent him from taking it), so William had 300 lanterns hung from the trees that lined the route, making Rotten Row the first road in England to be lit at night.

Kensington Palace
Kensington, W8

1. Date built: Jacobean/1689–90
2. Remodelled by: Sir Christopher Wren
3. Origin of name: Farm or homestead of the Anglo-Saxon family of Cynesige or Kensige
4. Family connection: Coppin/Nottingham/Crown
5. Historic events: Death of Queen Anne (1714), birth of future Queen Victoria (1819)

London Photographic Atlas: Page 53

Tel: (020) 7937 9561
www.hrp.org.uk

In 1689 William III and Queen Mary bought Nottingham House from William's Secretary of State, the Earl of Nottingham, and commissioned Christopher Wren to convert it for them into Kensington Palace for use as a private retreat. Home also to Queen Anne and Kings George I and George II, in more recent years it has been divided into a number of apartments allocated to various members of the royal family – a use of the palace which led the Duke of Windsor, formerly Edward VIII, to christen it "the aunt heap". Diana, Princess of Wales, lived here until her death in 1997.

King's Cross Station
King's Cross, N1

1. Date built: 1850–52
2. Architect: Lewis Cubitt
3. Origin of name: Close to the site of a
   cross erected to commemorate George IV
4. Built for: Great Northern Railway
5. Features: Twin trainsheds, 800 ft long and
   105 ft wide, originally intended as
   separate arrival and departure sides

London Photographic Atlas: Page 23

King's Cross was the biggest station in England when it opened in 1852, and was said to "wear a magnificent appearance" – so magnificent that the Chairman of the Great Northern Railway was accused by his shareholders of extravagance. He replied that it was "the cheapest building for what it contains and will contain, that can be pointed out in London". The tracks leaving the station pass under the Grand Union Canal, built from 1812-20 as the Regent's Canal and later incorporated in the Grand Union Canal network. The Battlebridge Basin, filled with colourful narrowboats, is surrounded by warehouses. One of these was built by Italian entrepreneur Carlo Gatti as an ice house – during the 19th century London's ice had to be collected from rivers and lakes and stored underground in specially constructed ice wells. Gatti was also the man who introduced ice cream to London.

Leicester Square
Covent Garden/Soho, WC2

1. Date laid out: 1670s
2. Laid out for: 2nd Earl of Leicester
3. Origin of name: 2nd Earl of Leicester, who built Leicester House here (1631–35)
4. Buildings: Odeon Cinema, Empire Cinema, Warner Cinema, Fanum House
5. Features: London's version of the Hollywood Walk of Fame

London Photographic Atlas: Page 58

Cinema moved into Leicester Square in the 1930s, taking over the theatres and music halls for which the square had previously been famous. The Empire Music Hall was demolished in 1927 and replaced a year later by the Empire Cinema. The Warner Village Cinema stands on the site of Daly's Theatre, the Hippodrome survives as a nightclub, and the Alhambra was replaced in 1936 by the sleek black lines of the Odeon. In 1870 the Alhambra had problems renewing its music hall licence after Wiry Sal had reportedly "raised her foot higher than her head several times towards the audience and had been much applauded".

London Central Mosque
St John's Wood, NW8

1. Date built: 1974–77
2. Architects: Frederick Gibberd & Partners
3. Dedicated to: Allah
4. Height of minaret: 150 ft
5. Denomination: Islam

London Photographic Atlas: Page 31

Tel: (020) 7724 3363
www.islamicculturalcentre.co.uk

The idea of a central London mosque was first mooted in the 1920s, but it was to be half a century before the idea was realized. The mosque was designed by Frederick Gibberd, who was also the architect of the adventurous Liverpool Roman Catholic Cathedral – the dome and minaret make a striking and eminently suitable addition to a park laid out for the Prince Regent, whose taste for eastern architecture led to the creation of the Brighton Pavilion. The mosque's Imam invites "all people of all religions to enter as a visitor, a student of Arabic culture, or a seeker after truth".

London Zoo
Regent's Park, NW1

1. Date opened: 1828
   (remodelled 1959 onwards)
2. Laid out by: Decimus Burton
   (remodelled by Sir Peter
   Shepheard and others)
3. Founded by: Zoological
   Society of London (Society
   founded 1826)
4. World firsts: Reptile house
   (1843), aquarium (1853),
   insect houses (1881)
5. Historic events: Penguin
   Books logo sketched at the
   new penguin pool by Edward
   Young (1932)

London Photographic Atlas:
Page 20

Tel: (020) 7722 3333
www.londonzoo.co.uk

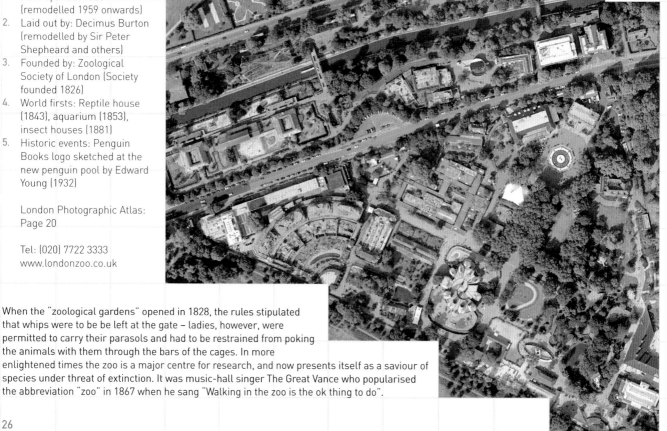

When the "zoological gardens" opened in 1828, the rules stipulated
that whips were to be be left at the gate – ladies, however, were
permitted to carry their parasols and had to be restrained from poking
the animals with them through the bars of the cages. In more
enlightened times the zoo is a major centre for research, and now presents itself as a saviour of
species under threat of extinction. It was music-hall singer The Great Vance who popularised
the abbreviation "zoo" in 1867 when he sang "Walking in the zoo is the ok thing to do".

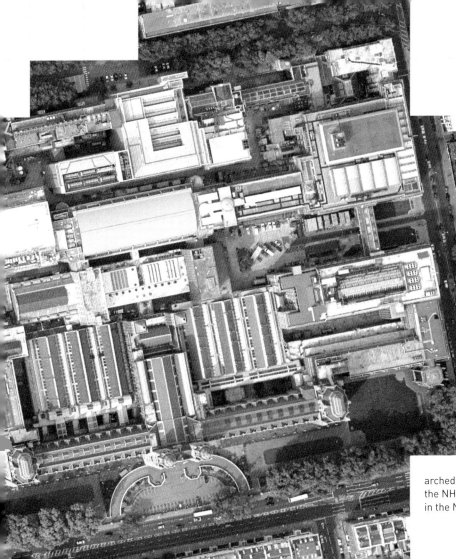

Natural History Museum and Science Museum
South Kensington, SW7

1. Date opened: 1881 (NHM)/1928 (East block building of SM)
2. Architect: Alfred Waterhouse (NHM)/Sir Richard Allison and others (SM)
3. Origin: Natural History Collection of the British Museum (NHM)/Science Collection of the V&A (SM)
4. Features (NHM): 675 ft terracotta façade, 4 acres of gallery space, 85 ft cast of diplodocus skeleton
5. Exhibits (SM): Seven floors on the history of science and technology, including an IMAX cinema

London Photographic Atlas: Page 66

Tel: (020) 7942 5011 (NHM)/(0870) 870 4771 (SM)
www.nhm.ac.uk/www.sciencemuseum.org.uk

This part of South Kensington is home to three of Britain's best-loved museums, two of which are seen here, and the area has been variously known as "Museumland" and "Albertropolis" since Prince Albert established several artistic and scientific institutions here in the wake of the Great Exhibition of 1851. The outstretched arms of the Natural History Museum face onto Cromwell Road, with the distinctive green arched roof of the Science Museum to the north. To the east of the NHM is the former Geological Museum, now incorporated in the NHM as the Earth Galleries.

27

Marble Arch
Mayfair, W1

1. Date built: 1827 (moved to present site 1851)
2. Designed by: John Nash
3. Origin: Based on the Arch of Constantine in Rome
4. Features: Three rooms within the arch, used as a police observation post from 1851–c. 1950
5. Historic events: Scene of an 1855 protest against the Sunday Trading Bill, attended by Karl Marx

London Photographic Atlas: Page 55

Oxford Street
St Giles Circus–Marble Arch, W1

1. Date developed: 1739 onwards
2. Developed by: Thomas Huddle and others
3. Origin of current name: Land on the north side owned by the Earls of Oxford
4. Length: c. 2 miles, following the route of the Roman road from Hampshire to Suffolk
5. Historic events: Thomas de Quincey bought his first dose of opium on Oxford Street

London Photographic Atlas: Page 43–46

Oxford Street is probably the most famous shopping street in the world, but things might have been very different if any of its earlier names had stuck – The Waye from Uxbridge, The King's Highway, Acton Road or Tyburn Way. The road does lead to Oxford, and was recorded in the 17th century as "The Road to Oxford", but the name was only consolidated after the Earl of Oxford acquired land to the north in 1713. He married Lady Henrietta Cavendish-Holles and their daughter married the Duke of Portland, giving rise to many of the local street names, including Portland Place, Henrietta Place, Cavendish Place and the circular, tree-filled Cavendish Square, seen to the north of Oxford Street in the photograph. Oxford Circus, once known as Regent Circus, marks the junction of Oxford Street with Regent Street, which is home to retailers such as Garrard & Co, Hamley's and Liberty.

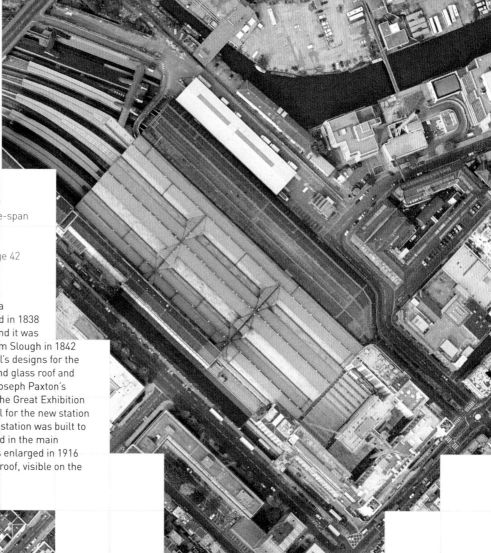

Paddington Station
Paddington, W2

1. Date built: 1851–54
2. Designed by: Isambard Kingdom Brunel (hotel by Philip Hardwick, 1868–74)
3. Origin of name: Farm or homestead of the Anglo-Saxon Padda or Paeda
4. Built for: Great Western Railway
5. Features: Brunel's original three-span trainshed (since enlarged)

London Photographic Atlas: Page 42

The first station at Paddington was a temporary wooden structure opened in 1838 to the west of the present station, and it was here that Queen Victoria arrived from Slough in 1842 after her first journey by rail. Brunel's designs for the new station, with its wrought iron and glass roof and cast-iron pillars, were inspired by Joseph Paxton's Crystal Palace which was used for the Great Exhibition of 1851, the same year that approval for the new station was given. A separate underground station was built to the north in 1863 (since incorporated in the main station), and Brunel's trainshed was enlarged in 1916 with the addition of a fourth arched roof, visible on the northern side of the station.

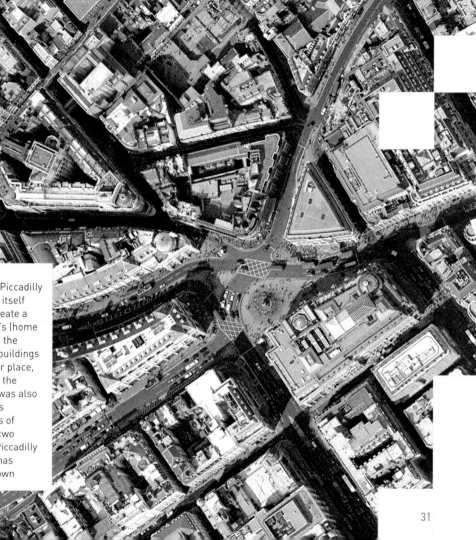

Piccadilly Circus
Soho, W1

1. Date formed: 1819
2. Architect: John Nash
3. Origin of name: The ruffs, or "pickadills" worn by the dandies who would promenade on Piccadilly in the 17th century
4. Buildings: Criterion Theatre, Trocadero, London Pavilion
5. Features: Illuminations (since c. 1910); Statue of Eros (1893), which in fact represents not Eros but the Angel of Christian Charity

London Photographic Atlas: Page 58

Piccadilly Circus was built as the intersection of Piccadilly with the newly constructed Regent Street, which itself was built as part of John Nash's grand plan to create a triumphal route from Carlton House in St James's (home of the Prince Regent) to Regent's Park. Although the junction was a crossroads it was surrounded by buildings with concave curved frontages, forming a circular place, or circus, known as Regent Circus – confusingly, the intersection of Regent Street with Oxford Street was also known as Regent Circus. Writing in 1888, Charles Dickens's son comments that "the eternal fitness of things has by this time vindicated itself, and the two circuses are known respectively as Regent and Piccadilly Circus". Since then the eternal fitness of things has vindicated itself more fully, and they are now known respectively as Oxford and Piccadilly Circus.

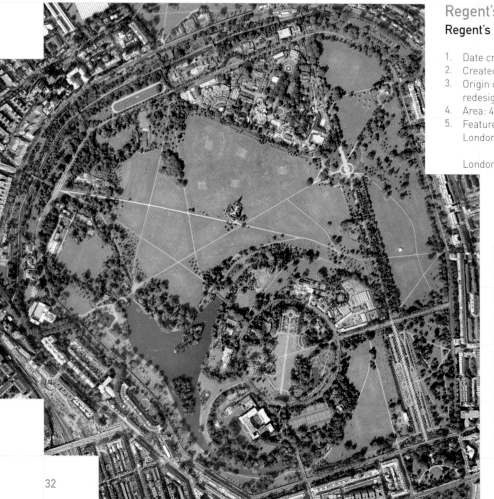

Regent's Park
Regent's Park, NW1

1. Date created: c. 1539 (redesigned 1811-26)
2. Created for: Henry VIII (redesigned by John Nash)
3. Origin of name: Originally Marylebone Park, it was redesigned for the Prince Regent (later George IV)
4. Area: 464 acres
5. Features: Queen Mary's Gardens, Open Air Theatre, London Zoo (see p. 26)

London Photographic Atlas: Page 32

Originally part of the Forest of Middlesex, Regent's Park is one of the many royal parks appropriated from the church by Henry VIII, and it remained Crown property until Charles I used it as a pledge for gunpowder with which to fight the Civil War. After Charles's execution, Marylebone Park, as it was then known, was sold at auction, including 16,297 trees, most of which were felled and used for the navy's ships. When the park once again became Crown property after the Restoration, most of it had been ploughed over and was being used for farmland. The farm leases expired in 1811 and the park was newly laid out by John Nash for the Prince Regent.

Royal Hospital, Chelsea
Chelsea, SW3

1. Date built: 1682–92
2. Architect: Sir Christopher Wren
3. Founded by: Charles II
4. Function: Retirement home for veteran soldiers
5. Historic events: The Duke Of Wellington lay in state here (1852)

London Photographic Atlas: Page 79

Tel: (020) 7730 0161

Legend has it that Charles II was persuaded to found the Chelsea Hospital by Nell Gwynn, who had been distressed by the sight of an old soldier begging on the King's Road. It is true that she was one of the hospital's first patrons, donating £200 to the cause, but it is more likely that Charles was emulating the example of Louis XIV's Hôtel des Invalides in Paris. The first of the famous Chelsea Pensioners took up residence in 1689, three years before the hospital was completed, and more than three centuries later, Chelsea Pensioners can still be identified by the same distinctive red uniform.

St James's Park

St James's, SW1

1. Date created: c. 1532 (opened to the public 17th century)
2. Created for: Henry VIII (opened to the public by Charles II)
3. Origin of name: Originally the grounds of St James's in the Fields, a hospital for leper women
4. Area: 93 acres
5. Features: The Canal, Birdcage Walk

London Photographic Atlas: Page 70

St James's is the oldest of the royal parks, having been drained by Henry VIII for use as a bowling alley and tilt yard attached to St James's Palace. James I kept a menagerie and an aviary in the park, pre-empting the fact that St James's is now an inner-city wildfowl reserve – the aviary, later enlarged by Charles II, stood close to what is now Birdcage Walk. Charles also extended the park by 36 acres, converted several small ponds into the strip of water known as the Canal (where he would often swim), and opened the park to the public.

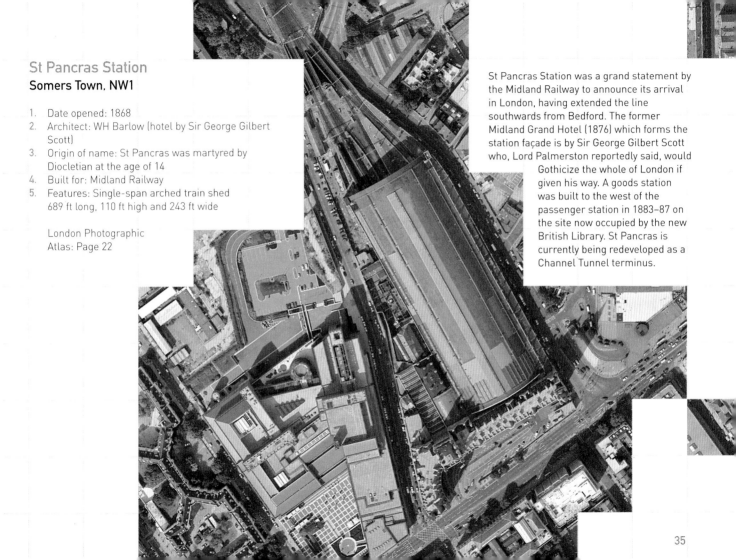

St Pancras Station
Somers Town, NW1

1. Date opened: 1868
2. Architect: WH Barlow (hotel by Sir George Gilbert Scott)
3. Origin of name: St Pancras was martyred by Diocletian at the age of 14
4. Built for: Midland Railway
5. Features: Single-span arched train shed 689 ft long, 110 ft high and 243 ft wide

London Photographic
Atlas: Page 22

St Pancras Station was a grand statement by the Midland Railway to announce its arrival in London, having extended the line southwards from Bedford. The former Midland Grand Hotel (1876) which forms the station façade is by Sir George Gilbert Scott who, Lord Palmerston reportedly said, would Gothicize the whole of London if given his way. A goods station was built to the west of the passenger station in 1883–87 on the site now occupied by the new British Library. St Pancras is currently being redeveloped as a Channel Tunnel terminus.

Seven Dials
Covent Garden, WC2

1. Date first developed: 1693–1710
2. Developer: Thomas Neale, Master of the Mint
3. Origin of name: The six-faced sundial (the seventh dial is formed by the circus itself)
4. Features: Replica of the original sundial, unveiled 1989
5. Historic events: Original sundial torn down in 1773 after a false rumour that money was buried beneath it!

London Photographic Atlas: Page 46

In 1694 diarist John Evelyn described the place "neare St Giles's where seven streetes make a starr from a Doric Pillar plac'd in the middle". The scene is much the same today, although the street names have changed and the pillar is a replica of the original, which has stood on the village green in Weybridge, Surrey, since 1882. The workings of the modern sundials are explained not by a diarist but by a recording artist of a different ilk – a plaque describing how to convert sundial time to GMT or BST is sponsored by one of Covent Garden's more famous residents, Dave Stewart of the Eurythmics.

Stamford Bridge Stadium
Fulham, SW6

1. Date opened: 1877 (rebuilt 1973-2001)
2. Rebuilt by: Fletcher Priest/Atherden Fuller Lang/KSS Design Ltd
3. Home club: Chelsea Football Club
4. Club founded: 1905 (stadium initially used by London Athletic Club)
5. Stadium capacity: 42,449

London Photographic Atlas: Page 158

Tel: (020) 7385 5545
www.chelseafc.co.uk

Stamford Bridge Stadium is twenty-eight years older than the club that plays here, having been officially opened on 28th April 1877 as an athletics stadium. Named after a bridge over Stanford Creek, it was designed by stadium architect Archibald Leitch (who also designed the first stadium at White Hart Lane). Ironically, the famous home of Chelsea FC is not actually in Chelsea, but in Fulham – and if Fulham FC had accepted an invitation to use Stamford Bridge, Chelsea FC might never have existed. The Mears brothers bought the stadium in 1904 with the intention of establishing a club there and, after Fulham had refused their invitation, they founded their own club the following year. The rest, as they say, is history.

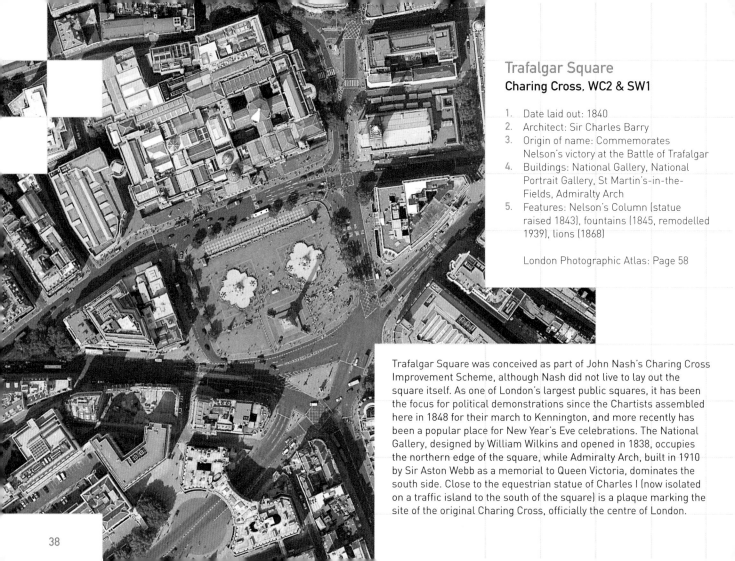

Trafalgar Square
Charing Cross, WC2 & SW1

1. Date laid out: 1840
2. Architect: Sir Charles Barry
3. Origin of name: Commemorates Nelson's victory at the Battle of Trafalgar
4. Buildings: National Gallery, National Portrait Gallery, St Martin's-in-the-Fields, Admiralty Arch
5. Features: Nelson's Column (statue raised 1843), fountains (1845, remodelled 1939), lions (1868)

London Photographic Atlas: Page 58

Trafalgar Square was conceived as part of John Nash's Charing Cross Improvement Scheme, although Nash did not live to lay out the square itself. As one of London's largest public squares, it has been the focus for political demonstrations since the Chartists assembled here in 1848 for their march to Kennington, and more recently has been a popular place for New Year's Eve celebrations. The National Gallery, designed by William Wilkins and opened in 1838, occupies the northern edge of the square, while Admiralty Arch, built in 1910 by Sir Aston Webb as a memorial to Queen Victoria, dominates the south side. Close to the equestrian statue of Charles I (now isolated on a traffic island to the south of the square) is a plaque marking the site of the original Charing Cross, officially the centre of London.

Victoria and Albert Museum (V&A)

South Kensington, SW7

1. Date opened: 1857/1899–1909
2. Architects: Cubitt, Fowke/Aston Webb
3. Founded by: Commissioners of the Great Exhibition
4. Exhibits: Sculpture, painting, photography, fashion, glass, ceramics, furniture, design
5. Features: Central tower 185 ft high, seven miles of gallery space

London Photographic Atlas: Page 66

Tel: (020) 7942 2000
www.vam.ac.uk

The V&A was the first of the great museums to open in South Kensington, after Prince Albert encouraged the Museum of Ornamental Art (previously the Museum of Manufactures) and the School of Design to relocate here. The two institutions were amalgamated as the South Kensington Museum, which opened in 1857 in temporary buildings that came to be known as the "Brompton Boilers". Forty-two years later, in the last important public duty of her reign, Queen Victoria laid the foundation stone of a new building and gave the museum its new name: the Victoria and Albert Museum.

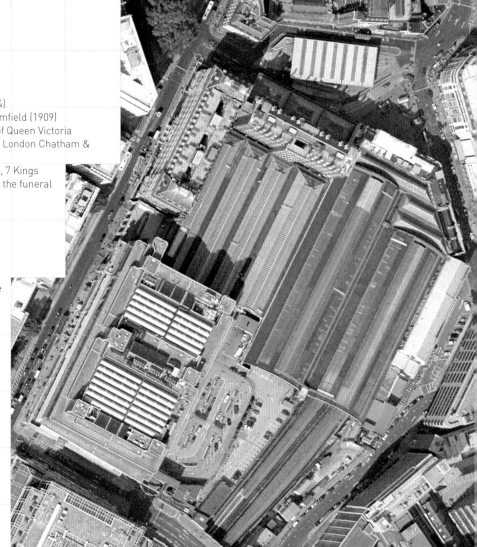

Victoria Station
Belgravia, SW1

1. Date built: 1860 & 62/1906-09 (united 1924)
2. Architects: Sir John Fowler (1862)/AW Blomfield (1909)
3. Origin of name: Opened during the reign of Queen Victoria
4. Built for: London Brighton & South Coast, London Chatham & Dover and Great Western Railways
5. Historic events: An Emperor and Empress, 7 Kings and more than 20 Princes arrived here for the funeral of Edward VII (1910)

London Photographic Atlas: Page 81

Victoria Station is actually two adjacent stations that were united in 1924. The first was built by the London Brighton & South Coast Railway in 1860 (the western side of the present station), followed two years later by the second, which was shared by the London Chatham & Dover and Great Western Railways. When the LBSCR rebuilt its station in 1906–09, the South Eastern & Chatham Railway, as it had become, followed suit and rebuilt the eastern side. A year after the 1923 Grouping of the Railways, the new Southern Railway finally united the stations by making an archway in the dividing wall and renumbering the platforms. Two large blocks of offices and shops were built over the LBSCR platforms in the 1980s, and the concourse was further unified in 1992, although the station still operates in two distinct halves.

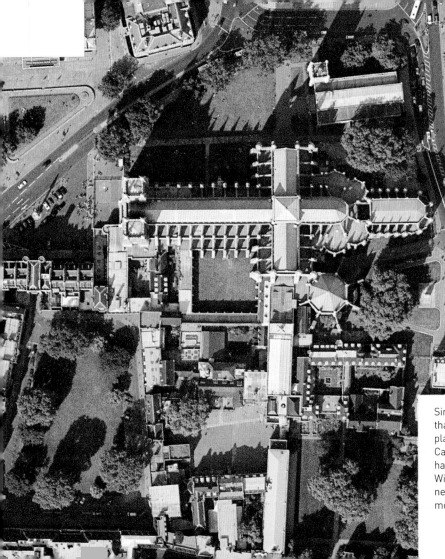

Westminster Abbey
Westminster, SW1

1. Date built: 1245–1532
2. Architects: Henry de Reyns and others
3. Dedicated to: St Peter
4. Height of west towers: 225 ft 4 in.
5. Denomination: Church of England

London Photographic Atlas: Page 70

Tel: (020) 7222 5152
www.westminster-abbey.org

Since St Peter apocryphally came here to dedicate the church that bore his name, what is now Westminster Abbey has played a large rôle in the history of England. Rebuilt by King Canute, Edward the Confessor and Henry III, the cathedral has seen the coronation of every English monarch since William the Conqueror (except for Edward V and Edward VIII, neither of whom was crowned) and the burial of every monarch in the 500 years between Henry III and George II.

Westminster Cathedral
Westminster, SW1

1. Date built: 1895-1903
2. Architect: John Francis Bentley
3. Dedicated to: Most Precious Blood of Our Lord
4. Height: 284 ft to top of cross
5. Denomination: Roman Catholic

London Photographic Atlas: Page 69

Tel: (020) 7798 9055
www.westminstercathedral.org.uk

Archbishop Herbert Vaughan commissioned Catholic convert John Francis Bentley to design Westminster Cathedral. Bentley's neo-Byzantine structure looks remarkable with its green domes and stripey walls, the stripes created by laying courses of Portland stone amid the 12.5 million terracotta-coloured bricks. The Campanile is dedicated to Edward the Confessor who, ironically, is buried close by in the Protestant Westminster Abbey.

city, docklands and east london

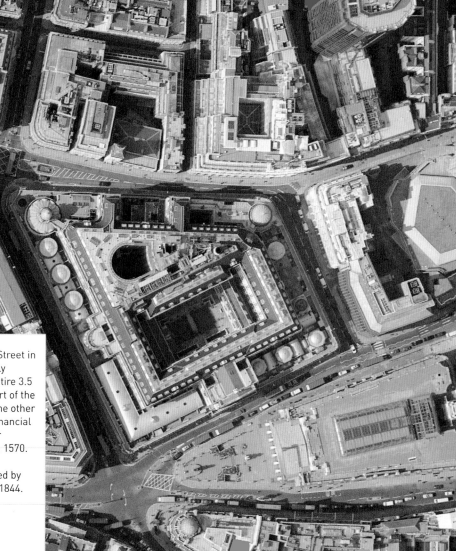

Bank of England
City, EC2

1. Date of present building: 1925–39
2. Architect: Sir Herbert Baker
3. Origin: Incorporated in 1694 by William III to finance the war against France
4. Features: Sir John Soane's 18th century "curtain wall"
5. Historic events: Mobbed during the Gordon Riots (1780), bombed during the Blitz (1941)

London Photographic Atlas: Page 50

Tel: (020) 7601 5545
www.bankofengland.co.uk

The Bank of England moved to Threadneedle Street in 1734, where the original building was gradually extended until Sir John Soane enclosed the entire 3.5 acre site in an outer "curtain" wall, the only part of the 18th-century building that survives today. On the other side of Threadneedle Street is an even older financial institution, the Royal Exchange, founded by Sir Thomas Gresham and opened by Elizabeth I in 1570. Since then the Royal Exchange has twice been destroyed by fire: the current building, designed by Edward Tite, was opened by Queen Victoria in 1844.

Barbican
City, EC2

1. Date redeveloped: 1955 onwards
2. Architects: Chamberlin, Powell & Bon
3. Origin of name: Medieval fortification, possibly a watch-tower
4. Area: 20 acres
5. Features: Three 400 ft, 43-storey blocks of flats; Barbican Arts Centre

London Photographic Atlas: Page 48

Tel: (020) 7638 4141
www.barbican.org.uk

The Barbican complex looks fairly picturesque from above, with its green areas, artificial lakes and the ancient church of St Giles Cripplegate (where Oliver Cromwell married) at its heart. The story on the ground is somewhat different, with a confusing tangle of concrete walkways linking twenty acres of buildings including Lauderdale, Cromwell and Shakespeare Towers, which were the tallest residential tower blocks in Europe when they were built. George Best memorably said that "it was an achievement to find my own front door in that concrete wasteland". Plans have been announced for a complete refurbishment to improve, amongst other things, ease of access and navigation around the site.

Canary Wharf
Poplar, E14

1. Date redeveloped: 1987–present
2. Developers: Olympia & York and others
3. Origin of name: Tomatoes and bananas were once landed here from the Canary Islands
4. Area of development: 71 acres
5. Features: One Canada Square, Britain's tallest building at 800 ft

London Photographic Atlas: Page 140

Tel: (020) 7418 2000
www.canarywharf.com

The redevelopment of Canary Wharf on the former West India Dock is the largest office development ever to have taken place in London, providing the equivalent of one-seventh of all the office space in the City at the time it was begun. The three landmark towers, visible from as far afield as Kent and Essex, form the grand centrepiece of the development, which also includes acres of lower-rise office buildings and Westferry Circus, a roundabout as big as Trafalgar Square.

East Ham Jewish Cemetery
East Ham, E6

1. Date consecrated: 1919
2. Laid out for: The United Synagogue
3. Origin of name: Recorded in the Domesday Book as Hame, meaning riverside land, since divided into East and West Ham
4. Number of graves: c. 40,000
5. Buried: Members of the Czech Pioneer Corps

London Photographic Atlas:
Page 244

The East Ham Jewish Cemetery was opened because the First World War and the ensuing flu epidemic had filled the other East End Jewish cemeteries. The first person to be buried in the new cemetery was a young Able-bodied Seaman, who died on 6th January 1919 while on active service and was buried here six days later. His grave, close to the trees on the northern boundary, is marked by a small box privet that is as old as the cemetery itself.

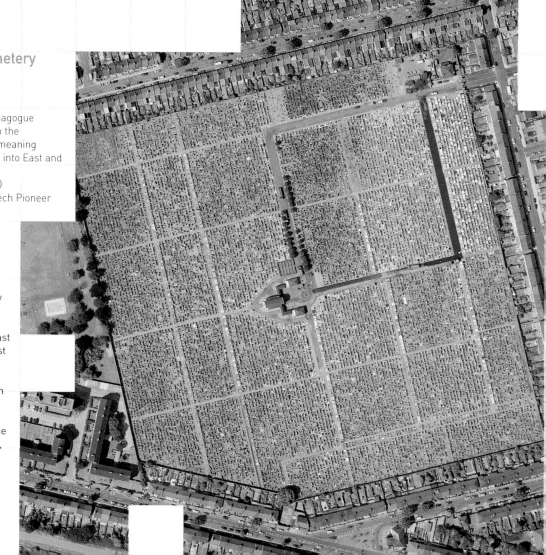

Ford Motor Works
Dagenham, RM9

1. Date built: 1929–31/2002–03
2. Built for: Ford Motor Company
3. Area: 473 acres
4. Production: 680,000 engines/year
5. Employees: 5,000

London Photographic Atlas: Page 247

Tel: (01277) 253000

Henry Ford's son Edsel cut the first sod of earth for the new works at Dagenham in May 1929, and the first vehicle (a model AA truck) was driven off the production line 17 months later, in October 1931. In May 2000, Ford announced that it was to end vehicle assembly at Dagenham and in February 2002 the last car rolled off the line (a Fiesta, auctioned for charity), marking the end of an era after the assembly of 10,980,368 vehicles. Dagenham's new rôle is as Ford's main centre for the engineering and manufacture of diesel engines, and a new engine plant due to be completed in 2003 will increase production to 900,000 engines per year.

Guildhall
City, EC2

1. Date built: 1411 onwards
2. Remodelled by: JB Bunning and Sir Horace Jones (19th century)
3. Origin of name: Anglo-Saxon "gild" meaning payment – the Guildhall was probably where citizens paid their taxes
4. Features: Effigies of the giants Gog and Magog by David Evans, Livery Hall by Sir Giles Gilbert Scott (1957)
5. Historic events: Venue for the trial of Lady Jane Grey, the 'nine days queen' (1553)

London Photographic Atlas: Page 49

Tel: (020) 7606 3030
www.cityoflondon.gov.uk

The Guildhall is the headquarters of the Corporation of London and has been the administrative centre of the City for nearly nine hundred years, being first mentioned in a survey of properties as early as 1128. The present 15th century building is the third largest civic hall in England, and was damaged in both the Great Fire of 1666 and the Blitz in 1941.

Hackney Marshes
Hackney, E5 & E9

1. Date drained: 1757
2. Purchased by London County Council, 1893
3. Origin of name: Disputed – from 'haccan' (to kill) and 'ey' (river) or 'Haca' (name) and 'eyot' (river island)
4. Area: 337 acres
5. Historic events: Danish Vikings sailed across the marshes up the River Lee (9th century)

London Photographic Atlas: Page 103

Even after they had been drained, Hackney Marshes remained subject to flooding until the 19th century when the Lee Navigation canal system was cut. The marshes became a popular place for hare and rabbit coursing, fishing, shooting, and bull-baiting, and they are still a popular place for outdoor activities in the 21st century, although football, cricket and golf have replaced bull-baiting and shooting, as evinced by the golf course and the huge number of football pitches bordered by the River Lee.

Inner and Middle Temple
City, EC4

1. Date built: 1185–1950s
2. Architects: Knights Templar – Maufe, Worthington
3. Origin of name: First built by the Knights of the Temple of Solomon of Jerusalem (Knights Templar)
4. Function: Knights' quarters, now the heart of the legal profession
5. Historic events: Premiere of Shakespeare's Twelfth Night (1602)

London Photographic Atlas: Page 60

www.innertemple.org.uk

Temple has been at the heart of the legal profession since the 13th century, when four Inns of Court were established as places where prospective lawyers could eat, sleep and study: even today all barristers must study at one of the four Inns. Temple comprises two Inns, Middle Temple and Inner Temple, which were originally hostels built by the Knights Templar as a hall of priests and a hall of knights. A few of the medieval buildings survive, including Temple Church (1185), but most of the current buildings were rebuilt during the 1950s after being heavily bombed in the Blitz.

Isle of Dogs
Isle of Dogs, E14

1. Date developed: 19th century
2. Developers: West India Company
3. Origin of name: Disputed – site of royal
    kennels or a corruption of the Flemish
    "dijk" (dyke)
4. Features: Canary Wharf, West India
    Docks, Millwall Dock, London Arena
5. Historic events: Windmills once stood
    on the western embankment to drain
    the land, hence the name Millwall (17th
    century)

London Photographic Atlas: Page 150

The Isle of Dogs, so-called for centuries, did
not actually become an island until 1805
when a canal was cut across the neck of the
peninsula as part of the West India Docks
development. The West India Docks (c. 54
acres) were followed in 1868 by the 36-acre
Millwall Dock to the south. The docks were
closed in 1980 and subsequently
redeveloped, leaving the Isle of Dogs as a
strange amalgam of council estates,
warehouse conversions, business parks and
office developments crowding the grassy
expanse of Mudchute, which was created by
the silt dumped after the dredging of
Millwall Dock. (For Millwall FC see p. 77.)

Limehouse Basin
Limehouse, E14

1. Date built: 1820s
2. Built for: The Regent's Canal and Dock Company
3. Origin of name: Site of lime oasts (kilns) dating back to the 14th century
4. Area: 10 acres of water
5. Historic events: Limehouse was London's first Chinatown (1890s–1950s)

London Photographic Atlas: Page 139

The Limehouse Basin (also known as the Regent's Canal Dock) was built by the Regent's Canal and Dock Company to accommodate ships at the eastern end of the Regent's Canal, which opened in 1820 linking Limehouse with Paddington, where the Regent's Canal joined the Grand Junction Canal (both were later incorporated in the Grand Union Canal). The dock, which is also linked to the Lee Navigation by the Limehouse Cut (running north-east from the basin), consisted of 10 acres of water, 4 acres of quays and docks, and a lock into the Thames. It ceased to operate commercially in 1969, since when it has been used only by leisure craft. The Limehouse Link tunnel now carries the A1203 beneath the basin, roughly following the curve of its northern edge – the road can be seen entering the tunnel to the west of the basin.

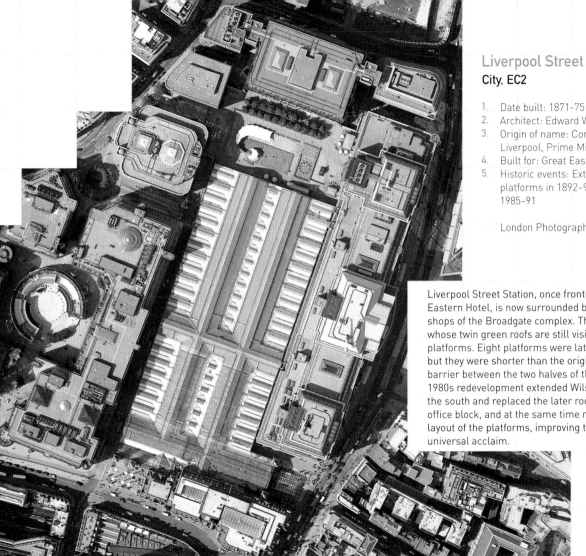

Liverpool Street Station
City, EC2

1. Date built: 1871-75
2. Architect: Edward Wilson
3. Origin of name: Commemorates Lord Liverpool, Prime Minister 1812–27
4. Built for: Great Eastern Railway
5. Historic events: Extended by eight platforms in 1892–94, redeveloped in 1985–91

London Photographic Atlas: Page 50

Liverpool Street Station, once fronted by the Great Eastern Hotel, is now surrounded by the offices and shops of the Broadgate complex. The original station, whose twin green roofs are still visible, consisted of ten platforms. Eight platforms were later added alongside, but they were shorter than the originals, creating a barrier between the two halves of the station. The 1980s redevelopment extended Wilson's original roof to the south and replaced the later roof with an overhead office block, and at the same time rationalized the layout of the platforms, improving the station to almost universal acclaim.

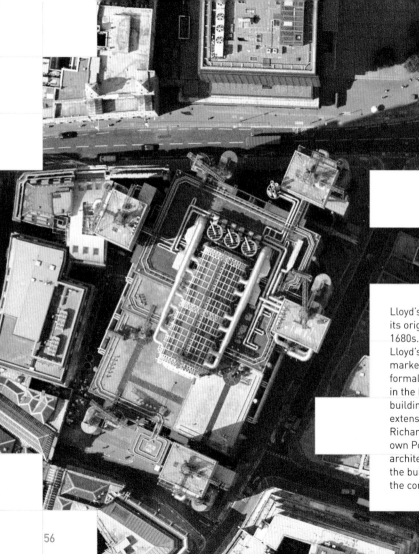

Lloyd's Building
City, EC3

1. Date of present building: 1986
2. Architect: Sir Richard Rogers
3. Origin of name: Edward Lloyd's 17th-century coffee-house
4. Features: The Lutine Bell
5. Historic events: The building was sold in 1996 to a German financial institution and is now rented by Lloyd's

London Photographic Atlas: Page 50

Lloyd's of London is now the world's largest insurance market, but its origins lie in a humble coffee house run by Edward Lloyd in the 1680s. Sea captains, shipowners and merchants would meet at Lloyd's, and the coffee house soon became an informal marketplace for buying and selling marine insurance. In 1771 a formal society was established, which eventually found premises in the Royal Exchange, and in 1928 Lloyd's moved into its own building on the present site (later linked by bridge to a 1950s extension). The site was redeveloped in eye-catching style by Sir Richard Rogers during the 1980s with a building reminiscent of his own Pompidou Centre in Paris, providing an interesting architectural contrast with the centuries-old traditions of Lloyd's – the building is attended by porters in waiters' livery, a reminder of the company's coffee-house origins.

London, Southwark and Alexandra Bridges
City-Southwark, EC4-SE1

1. Date built: 1912-21 (Southwark)/1863-66 (Alexandra)/1967-72 (Lond)
2. Architects: Sir Ernest George (Southwark)/John Hawkshaw (Alexandra)/ Lord Holford (Lond)
3. Engineers: Mott & Hay (Southwark)/John Wolfe-Barry (Alexandra)/Mott, Hay & Anderson (Lond)
4. Dimensions: 517 ft long, 55 ft wide (Southwark)/800 ft long, 105 ft wide (Lond)
5. Type of bridge: 5-span steel arch (Southwark)/5-span plate girder (Alexandra)/3-span concrete cantilever (Lond)

London Photographic Atlas: Page 61

London Bridge is the oldest and the newest of the bridges in this picture – the first London Bridge was built during the Roman occupation, while the present one was built to replace John Rennie's bridge which now spans a lake in Arizona. The first Southwark Bridge (1814–19, also by John Rennie), played a vital part in the growth of villages to the south of London. Equally important to the growth of the city was the arrival of the railways: Alexandra Bridge, better known as the Cannon Street Railway Bridge, was built for the South Eastern Railway at the same time as Cannon Street Station and designed by the same architect, John Hawkshaw.

Royal Group of Docks
Royal Docks, E16

1. Date opened: 1855, 1880 and 1921
2. Built by: St Katharine's Dock Co., London Dock Co. and Port of London Authority
3. Origin of name: The group consists of the Royal Victoria, Royal Albert and King George V docks
4. Area: 245 acres with nearly 9 miles of quay
5. Historic events: The 35,655 ton P&O liner **Mauretania** docked here in 1939

London Photographic Atlas: Page 244

The first of the Royal Group to be built was the Royal Victoria, to the west, which was opened by Prince Albert in 1855. Soil from the excavation was used to consolidate the marshes of Battersea Fields in order to create Battersea Park (p. 70), which was opened four years later. Victoria Dock was such a success that it was extended to the east to form the Royal Albert Dock, the largest of the group. King George V Dock, to the south of the Royal Albert, was begun in 1912 but the First World War delayed the work and it was not opened until 1921. In 1981, only sixty years after the last of the Royal Group opened, all three were closed, the quayside subsequently providing space for the runway of London City Airport.

City Airport
Royal Docks, E16

1. Date opened: 1987
2. Operated by: London City Airport Ltd
3. Air transport movements (2000): 50,049
4. Passengers (2000): 1,583,843
5. Runway: 10/28, 3,934 ft (lengthened 1992)

London Photographic Atlas: Page 244

Tel: (020) 7646 0000
www.londoncityairport.com

The runway of London City Airport lies on what was once the bustling centre quay between the Royal Albert and King George V docks, both at one time crowded with ships waiting to unload. The first meeting between the developers, Mowlem Construction, and the London Docklands Development Corporation took place early in 1981, but work didn't begin until April 1986 after a public inquiry over planning permission and wrangling between the Port of London Authority and the LDDC over ownership of the freehold. Commercial services began on 26th October 1987 and the airport was officially opened by the Queen just over a week later on 5th November. In 1992 the runway was lengthened to accommodate larger aircraft, and in 1998 the maximum permitted number of flights was doubled, rising to 73,000.

St Katharine Docks
Tower Hamlets, E1

1. Date built: 1827-28
2. Designed by: Thomas Telford
   (architect Philip Hardwick)
3. Origin of name: Once the site
   of St Katharine's Hospital
   (she of the Catherine Wheel)
4. Area: 23 acres
5. Historic events: Heavily
   bombed 1940, closed in 1968
   and subsequently
   redeveloped by Taylor
   Woodrow

London Photographic Atlas:
Page 63

Tel: (020) 7481 8350
www.stkaths.co.uk

The Royal Foundation of St Katharine was established here in 1148, and the Foundation's church was demolished in 1825 to make way for the docks. Telford's revolutionary design of linked basins provided an exceptional length of quayside for a relatively small enclosure of water. The only surviving warehouse from Telford's docks is the Ivory House, now at the centre of the marina, which in its day handled not only ivory but also perfume, wine and shells. Legend has it that the founder of a certain multinational corporation used to collect discarded scallop shells here, which years later provided him with the name and logo of his organization, Shell Oil.

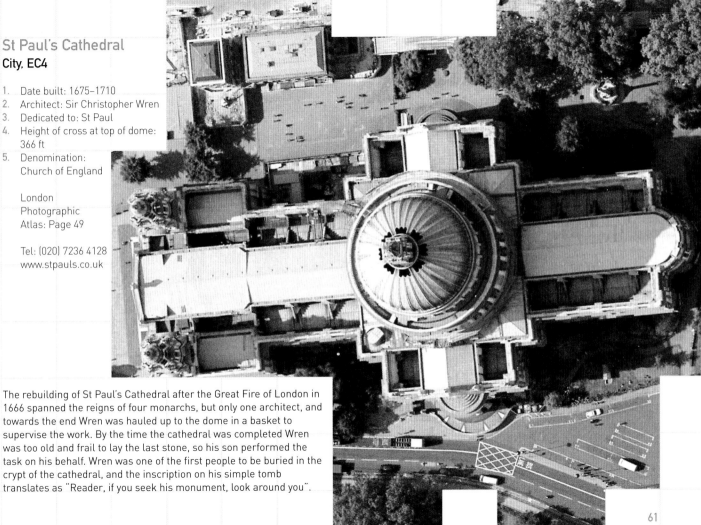

St Paul's Cathedral
City, EC4

1. Date built: 1675–1710
2. Architect: Sir Christopher Wren
3. Dedicated to: St Paul
4. Height of cross at top of dome: 366 ft
5. Denomination: Church of England

London
Photographic
Atlas: Page 49

Tel: (020) 7236 4128
www.stpauls.co.uk

The rebuilding of St Paul's Cathedral after the Great Fire of London in 1666 spanned the reigns of four monarchs, but only one architect, and towards the end Wren was hauled up to the dome in a basket to supervise the work. By the time the cathedral was completed Wren was too old and frail to lay the last stone, so his son performed the task on his behalf. Wren was one of the first people to be buried in the crypt of the cathedral, and the inscription on his simple tomb translates as "Reader, if you seek his monument, look around you".

Smithfield Market
City, EC1

1. Date of present buildings: 1851-66/1963
2. Architect: Sir Horace Jones/City of London Corporation
3. Origin of name: "Smoothfield", a medieval horse market
4. Area: c. 10 acres
5. Historic events: Poultry section (green roof) burned down in 1958 and reopened in 1963

London Photographic Atlas: Page 48

Tel: (020) 7236 8734

Over nine centuries Smithfield has been a horse fair, a venue for sporting events and royal tournaments, the site of St Bartholomew's Fair, a jousting arena, a public execution ground, and finally London's biggest meat market. During the 19th century the live cattle market was moved to Islington and the present market buildings were erected, but for several hundred years before that live cattle were herded into the City and slaughtered here. Often the livestock stampeded, sometimes taking refuge in shops, which is thought to be the origin of the phrase "a bull in a china shop".

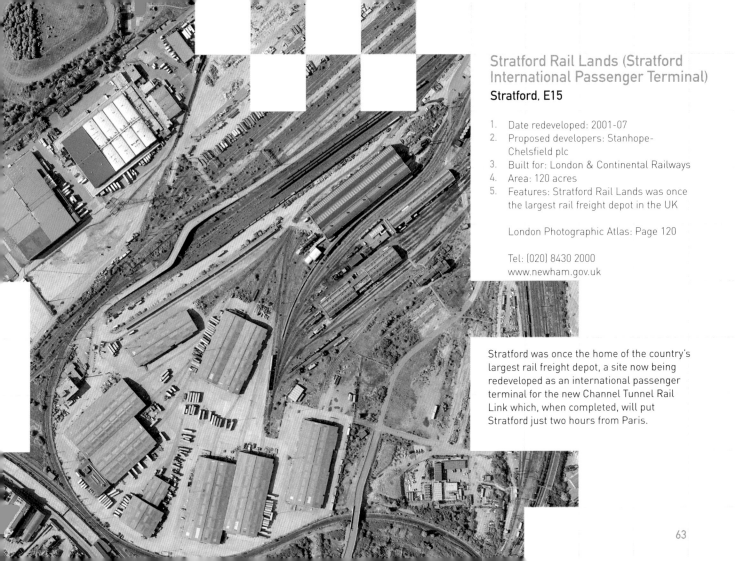

Stratford Rail Lands (Stratford International Passenger Terminal)
Stratford, E15

1. Date redeveloped: 2001-07
2. Proposed developers: Stanhope-Chelsfield plc
3. Built for: London & Continental Railways
4. Area: 120 acres
5. Features: Stratford Rail Lands was once the largest rail freight depot in the UK

London Photographic Atlas: Page 120

Tel: (020) 8430 2000
www.newham.gov.uk

Stratford was once the home of the country's largest rail freight depot, a site now being redeveloped as an international passenger terminal for the new Channel Tunnel Rail Link which, when completed, will put Stratford just two hours from Paris.

Stratford Market Depot (London Underground)
Stratford, E15

1. Date opened: 2000
2. Architect: Chris Wilkinson Architects
3. Origin: Former fruit and vegetable market
4. Dimensions: 190 m x 110 m, 15 m high
5. Awards: Civic Trust, Financial Times Design, RIBA Commercial Architecture, BCI, and Structural Steel Design Awards

London Photographic Atlas: Page 131

Tel: 0845 330 9880
www.thetube.com

The sheer scale of the award-winning Stratford Market Depot can only be appreciated by comparing the size of the graceful parallelogram-shaped aluminium roof with the length of the eighteen tube trains parked alongside. The depot will be home to 33 of the 59 trains serving the Jubilee Line extension between Stratford and Stanmore, the remainder of the fleet being based at Neasden. 11,889 metres of track were laid in the construction of the Stratford Depot – almost a third of all the track laid for the entire Jubilee Line extension.

Thames Barrier
Silvertown-Charlton, E16-SE7

1. Date built: 1975–82
2. Engineers: Rendell, Palmer & Tritton
3. Span: 4 large and 6 small gates totalling 520 m
4. Dimensions: Each of the four large gates is 61 m wide and weighs 3,000 tonnes
5. Historic events: In October 1997 a 3,000-ton ship hit the barrier in thick fog

London Photographic Atlas: Page 252

Tel: (020) 8305 4188

At the opening ceremony in 1983 the Queen described the Thames Barrier as the Eighth Wonder of the World, and it is not only a stunning piece of architecture but a remarkable feat of engineering, most of which is hidden under water. Between the gleaming machine housings are ten retractable steel gates which lie in concrete sills on the river bed and take about thirty minutes to raise – the four main gates are each as high as a five storey building and as wide as the opening of Tower Bridge. Thames tides are rising by approximately two feet every century and the Barrier has been raised in earnest several times since it was completed – to date it has always stopped the tide, achieving what Canute could not.

Tower 42 (NatWest Tower)
City, EC2

1. Date built: 1971-80
2. Architects: R. Seifert & Partners
3. Height: 610 ft (186 m)
4. Origin of name: 42 floors of office space
5. Features: Originally the NatWest Tower, its footprint is the shape of the NatWest Bank's logo

London Photographic Atlas: Page 50

Tel: (020) 7877 7777
www.tower42.com

When it was completed as the NatWest Tower in 1980, Tower 42 took over from the BT Tower as Britain's tallest building, and remained so until the completion of Canada Tower at Canary Wharf a decade later. It is apt that such a monument to commerce should be built on the site of Thomas Gresham's house – Gresham was financial adviser to Elizabeth I and founder of the Royal Exchange. The NatWest Tower was taken over during the 1990s by a consortium which signalled the change of name and ownership by opening the Vertigo[42] champagne bar on the 42nd floor.

Tower Bridge
Tower Hamlets-Bermondsey, E1-SE1

1. Date built: 1886–94
2. Architect: Sir Horace Jones
3. Engineer: John Wolfe-Barry
4. Length: 800 ft - opening span 260 ft,
   side spans 2 x 270 ft
5. Type of bridge: Bascule, with side spans
   suspended

London Photographic Atlas: Page 63

Tel: (020) 7430 3761
www.towerbridge.org.uk

Although it is only just over one hundred years old,
Tower Bridge is, with the possible exception of Big Ben,
London's most famous landmark, and is so closely
identified with the capital that it is often confused (in
name, not profile) with London Bridge. Tower Bridge
was designed to be in architectural harmony with its
ancient namesake, the Tower of London, and has a
stone-clad steel frame to support the enormous weight
of the lifting arms of the roadway, known as bascules,
from the French word for see-saw. Bascule itself
comes from two older French words, 'battre', meaning
to bump, and 'cul', meaning backside.

Tower of London
Tower Hamlets, EC3

1. Date built: c. 1067–1285
2. Built for: William I - Edward I
3. Area: 18 acres
4. Dimensions of keep: 107 ft x 118 ft, 90 ft high
5. Purpose: At various times a fortress, palace, prison, execution site, armoury, mint, observatory and zoo

London Photographic Atlas: Page 63

Tel: (020) 7680 9004
www.tower-of-london.com

The Tower of London is officially a royal palace, although it is far better known as a prison – one American author even noted that the Tower "is to poisoning, hanging, beheading, regicide and torture what the Yankee Stadium is to baseball". The Tower's first prisoner was Ralf Flambard, Bishop of Durham, who was also one of the few to escape, lowering a rope from a window after getting the guards drunk. The last, 840 years later in 1941, was Rudolf Hess, although new evidence suggests that the man who then spent the rest of his life in Spandau jail may have been an impostor and not the real Hess.

south of the river

Battersea Park
Battersea, SW11

1. Date opened: 1853
2. Laid out by: Sir James Pennethorne
3. Origin of name: Badric's or Batrice' Island
4. Area: 198 acres
5. Features: Peace Pagoda (1985), Children's Zoo (1951), Festival of Britain Gardens (1951)

London Photographic Atlas: Page 1

Tel: (020) 8871 7534
www.wandsworth.gov.uk/batterseapa

Battersea Park was the second of the great Victorian municipal parks, opening eight years after Victoria Park and laid out by the same designer, Sir James Pennethorne. Prior to that Battersea Fields had been a series of low marshes, streams and ditches: th soil used for consolidating this marshland came from the excavation of the Royal Victoria Dock further downriver (see p. 58–59). The Peace Pagoda on the riverfront was accepted as a gift from Japanese Buddhists by the Greater London Counc. in 1984 as part of their Peace Year. It was completed in 1985 and is one of 70 such pagodas to be built around the world in the name of peace.

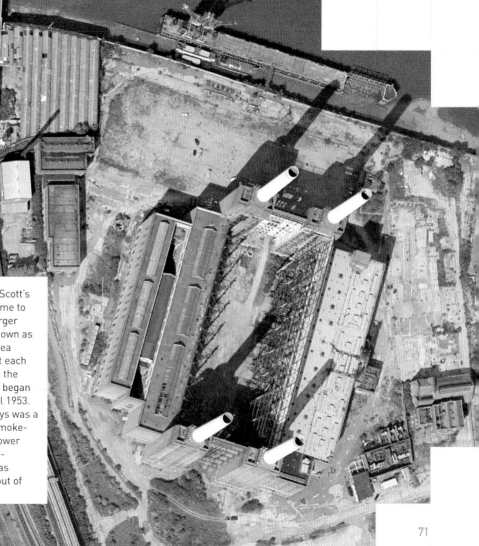

Battersea Power Station
Battersea, SW8

1. Date opened: 1933 (construction completed 1953)
2. Architect: Sir Giles Gilbert Scott
3. Decommissioned: 1983
4. Features: Four 300 ft fluted chimneys
5. Historic events: Featured on the cover of Pink Floyd's "Animals" with an inflatable pig attached to one of the chimneys (1977)

London Photographic Atlas: Page 160

Battersea Power Station is in a sorrier state than Scott's other riverside power station at Bankside, now home to the Tate Modern (p. 98-99), and both are rather larger than his most familiar creation, the K6 – better known as the classic red telephone box. Station A of Battersea Power Station opened in 1933 with one chimney at each end, and the station was later doubled in size with the addition of Station B to the east which, although it began generating power in 1948, was not completed until 1953. The smoke that once issued from the four chimneys was a pristine white, having been "washed" by special smoke-cleaning apparatus. In 1988, five years after the power station had been decommissioned, the site was re-opened for development as a leisure park but it was abandoned again in 1991 after the developer ran out of money.

Biggin Hill Airport
Biggin Hill, Kent

1. Date opened: 1917
2. Operated by: Regional Airports Ltd
3. Air transport movements (2000): 1,323
4. Passengers (2000): 6,168
5. Runways: 03/21 (5,932 ft) & 11/29 (2,677 ft)

England Photographic Atlas: Page 195

Tel: (01959) 571111
www.bigginhillairport.com

Biggin Hill is most famous as "the Battle of Britain airfield", and deservedly so – by the middle of 1943, under the control of Fighter Command, aircraft based at Biggin Hill had destroyed 1,000 enemy planes, a record that was never beaten. The main runway was extended in 1957 to accommodate jet aircraft but only two years later the RAF ceased flying from Biggin Hill, partly because airspace south of London was becoming increasingly crowded. Since then the airfield has been used by light aircraft and executive flights, with scheduled services to northern France. The number of air transport movements is far outnumbered by nearly 100,000 club and private flights each year.

Clapham Common
Clapham, SW4

1. Date drained: 1760
2. Created by: Christopher Baldwin
3. Origin of name: Disputed – "homestead belonging to Clope" (or Cloppa), or simply "homestead on the hill"
4. Area: 220 acres
5. Historic events: Samuel Pepys (from 1700–03) and William Wilberforce (19th century) owned houses overlooking the common

London Photographic Atlas: Page 176

After Clapham Marsh had been drained to become Clapham Common the land was planted and constantly improved, to the point where Thackeray felt moved to write of it that "of all the pretty suburbs that still adorn our metropolis there are few that exceed in charm Clapham Common".

Clapham Junction
Battersea, SW11

1. Date opened: 1863
2. Used by (1922): London & South Western, London Brighton & South Coast, and Southern Railways
3. Origin: A signal box was sited here in 1839, 24 years before the station opened
4. Features: Once the busiest rail junction in the world with more than 2,500 trains per day
5. Historic events: 56 people died here in a crash resulting from poor signalling (1988)

London Photographic Atlas: Page 175

At one time Clapham Junction was just that – a rail junction with a signal box. Later a station developed at the junction, serving the lines that converged on Victoria and Waterloo from the north-west, south and west. Stations with the word 'junction' in their name caused long-standing confusion on the railways because some of them were named after the location of the junction and some of them were named after the destination which the junction led to. Clapham Junction added to the confusion because, although it is named after its location, it is not actually in Clapham but in Battersea.

Crystal Palace Park
Sydenham, SE19 & SE20

1. Date opened: 1854
2. Laid out by: Crystal Palace Company
3. Origin of name: Laid out around the Crystal Palace, which was moved here from Hyde Park after the Great Exhibition of 1851
4. Area: 200 acres
5. Historic events: The Crystal Palace itself burned to the ground on 30th November 1936

London Photographic Atlas: Page 274

The Crystal Palace was a huge iron and glass exhibition hall designed by Joseph Paxton, based on the conservatory at Chatsworth House (also by Paxton). It was erected in Hyde Park for the duration of the Great Exhibition of 1851 and afterwards re-erected at Sydenham by the Crystal Palace Company, which also laid out the park with lakes and gardens, two 90-metre fountains, a zoo, a cricket ground and a sports arena. The Crystal Palace burned to the ground in 1936, despite the attentions of 90 fire appliances, but the park survived and is now renowned for its sports facilities.

Cutty Sark
Greenwich, SE10

1. Date launched: 1869 (opened to the public 1957)
2. Designed by: Hercules Linton
3. Origin of name: A short shift, or dress, as worn by the witch Nannie in Robert Burns's poem "Tam O'Shanter"
4. Dimensions: Length 212 ft, beam 36 ft, draft 21 ft
5. Figurehead: The witch Nannie clutching the tail of the horse on which Tam is trying to escape

London Photographic Atlas: Page 166

Tel: (020) 8858 3445
www.cuttysark.org.uk

Cutty Sark was built as an express challenge to the dominance of the clipper Thermopylae, but by the time the Cutty Sark was launched the tea trade was already being lost to steam ships, which could use the shorter route via the newly-opened Suez Canal. Cutty Sark made just eight voyages in the tea trade and it was as a wool clipper that the ship made its name, returning from New South Wales in just 69 days. Captain Wilfred Downman bought and restored the Cutty Sark to its original clipper rig in 1922, and in 1936 his widow presented the ship to the Thames Nautical Training College. The London County Council subsequently set up a sponsorship scheme to preserve the ship, which was placed in dry dock in Greenwich in 1954, further restored, and opened to the public in 1957.

The Den

South Bermondsey, SE16

1. Date officially opened: 4th August 1993
2. Architects: Thorburns
3. Home club: Millwall FC (nicknamed the Lions, hence the name "The Den")
4. Club founded: 1885, as Millwall Rovers
5. Stadium capacity: 20,146

London Photographic Atlas: Page 148

Tel: (020) 7232 1222
www.millwallfc.co.uk

Millwall FC was originally formed as Millwall Rovers by workers at Morton's jam factory on the Isle of Dogs (p. 53), later changing its name to Millwall Athletic and then plain Millwall. As many of the factory workers were Scottish, white and blue were chosen as the club colours. The name Millwall stems from the line of windmills that once stood on the western embankment of the Isle of Dogs to drain the low-lying marshland, and the club kept the name even when it relocated south of the river to Cold Blow Lane in 1910. By then the club was nicknamed the Lions, and the stadium became known as The Den. Millwall moved again in 1993, to a £16 m all-seater stadium known at first as the New Den, opened on 4th August that year by the late John Smith MP.

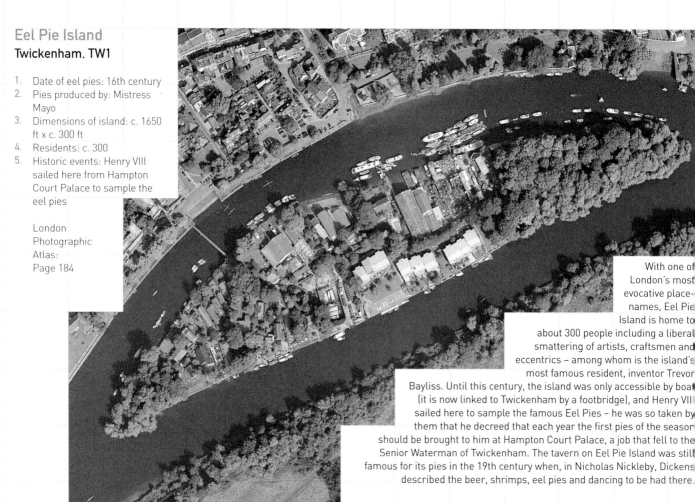

Eel Pie Island
Twickenham, TW1

1. Date of eel pies: 16th century
2. Pies produced by: Mistress Mayo
3. Dimensions of island: c. 1650 ft x c. 300 ft
4. Residents: c. 300
5. Historic events: Henry VIII sailed here from Hampton Court Palace to sample the eel pies

London
Photographic
Atlas:
Page 184

With one of London's most evocative place-names, Eel Pie Island is home to about 300 people including a liberal smattering of artists, craftsmen and eccentrics – among whom is the island's most famous resident, inventor Trevor Bayliss. Until this century, the island was only accessible by boat (it is now linked to Twickenham by a footbridge), and Henry VII sailed here to sample the famous Eel Pies – he was so taken by them that he decreed that each year the first pies of the season should be brought to him at Hampton Court Palace, a job that fell to the Senior Waterman of Twickenham. The tavern on Eel Pie Island was still famous for its pies in the 19th century when, in Nicholas Nickleby, Dickens described the beer, shrimps, eel pies and dancing to be had there.

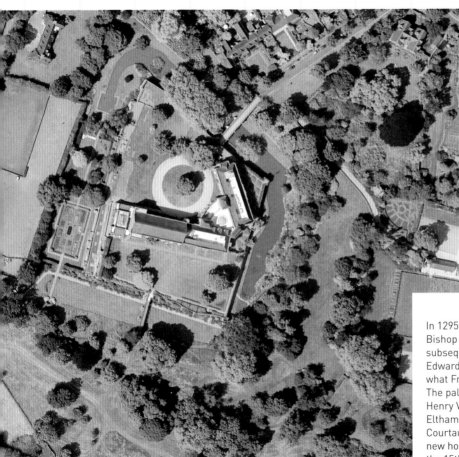

Eltham Palace
Eltham, SE9

1. Date built: 13th–15th century/1931-37
2. Architects: Bishop Bek (extended by the Crown)/Seeley & Paget
3. Origin of name: Elta's village
4. Family connection: Bishop Bek/Crown/Courtauld
5. Features: Great Hall (c. 1475), recreations of the Courtaulds' 1930s décor and furniture

London Photographic Atlas: Page 260

Tel: (020) 8294 2548
www.english-heritage.org.uk

In 1295 the Manor of Eltham passed to Antony Bek, Bishop of Durham, who rebuilt the Manor House. He subsequently passed it to the Prince of Wales (later Edward II), who extended the buildings further to create what Froissart described as "a very magnificent palace". The palace was further improved by successive kings, Henry VIII being the last monarch to spend much time at Eltham. In 1931 a lease was granted to Stephen Courtauld, who restored the medieval Great Hall, built a new house and redesigned the gardens, which include the 15th century bridge across what used to be the moat.

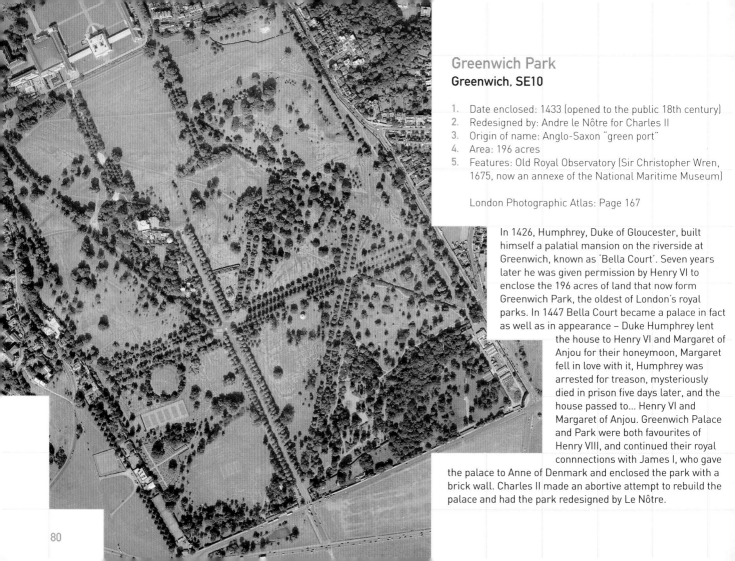

Greenwich Park
Greenwich, SE10

1. Date enclosed: 1433 (opened to the public 18th century)
2. Redesigned by: Andre le Nôtre for Charles II
3. Origin of name: Anglo-Saxon "green port"
4. Area: 196 acres
5. Features: Old Royal Observatory (Sir Christopher Wren, 1675, now an annexe of the National Maritime Museum)

London Photographic Atlas: Page 167

In 1426, Humphrey, Duke of Gloucester, built himself a palatial mansion on the riverside at Greenwich, known as 'Bella Court'. Seven years later he was given permission by Henry VI to enclose the 196 acres of land that now form Greenwich Park, the oldest of London's royal parks. In 1447 Bella Court became a palace in fact as well as in appearance – Duke Humphrey lent the house to Henry VI and Margaret of Anjou for their honeymoon, Margaret fell in love with it, Humphrey was arrested for treason, mysteriously died in prison five days later, and the house passed to... Henry VI and Margaret of Anjou. Greenwich Palace and Park were both favourites of Henry VIII, and continued their royal connnections with James I, who gave the palace to Anne of Denmark and enclosed the park with a brick wall. Charles II made an abortive attempt to rebuild the palace and had the park redesigned by Le Nôtre.

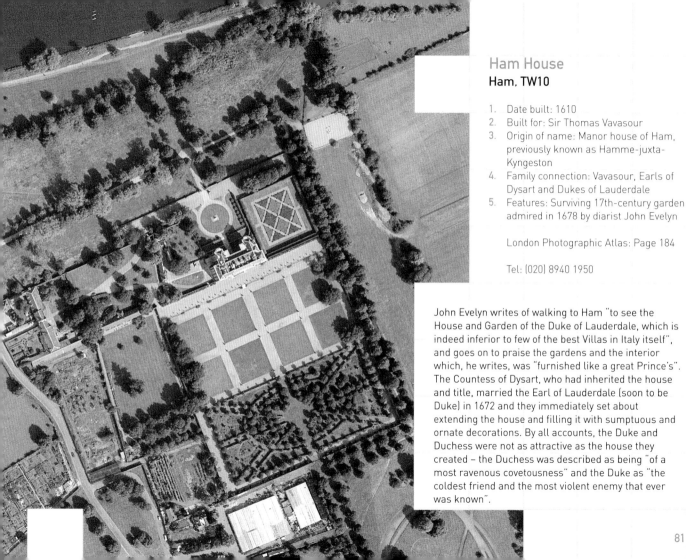

Ham House
Ham, TW10

1. Date built: 1610
2. Built for: Sir Thomas Vavasour
3. Origin of name: Manor house of Ham, previously known as Hamme-juxta-Kyngeston
4. Family connection: Vavasour, Earls of Dysart and Dukes of Lauderdale
5. Features: Surviving 17th-century garden admired in 1678 by diarist John Evelyn

London Photographic Atlas: Page 184

Tel: (020) 8940 1950

John Evelyn writes of walking to Ham "to see the House and Garden of the Duke of Lauderdale, which is indeed inferior to few of the best Villas in Italy itself", and goes on to praise the gardens and the interior which, he writes, was "furnished like a great Prince's". The Countess of Dysart, who had inherited the house and title, married the Earl of Lauderdale (soon to be Duke) in 1672 and they immediately set about extending the house and filling it with sumptuous and ornate decorations. By all accounts, the Duke and Duchess were not as attractive as the house they created – the Duchess was described as being "of a most ravenous covetousness" and the Duke as "the coldest friend and the most violent enemy that ever was known".

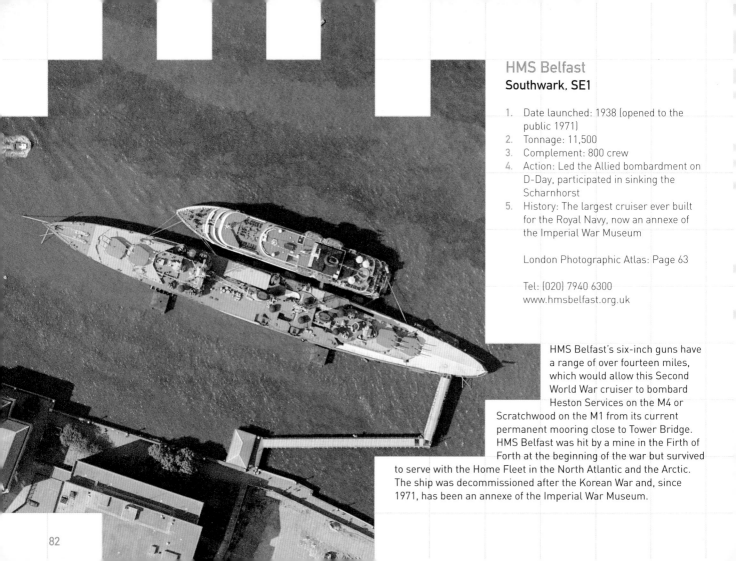

HMS Belfast
Southwark, SE1

1. Date launched: 1938 (opened to the public 1971)
2. Tonnage: 11,500
3. Complement: 800 crew
4. Action: Led the Allied bombardment on D-Day, participated in sinking the Scharnhorst
5. History: The largest cruiser ever built for the Royal Navy, now an annexe of the Imperial War Museum

London Photographic Atlas: Page 63

Tel: (020) 7940 6300
www.hmsbelfast.org.uk

HMS Belfast's six-inch guns have a range of over fourteen miles, which would allow this Second World War cruiser to bombard Heston Services on the M4 or Scratchwood on the M1 from its current permanent mooring close to Tower Bridge. HMS Belfast was hit by a mine in the Firth of Forth at the beginning of the war but survived to serve with the Home Fleet in the North Atlantic and the Arctic. The ship was decommissioned after the Korean War and, since 1971, has been an annexe of the Imperial War Museum.

Imperial War Museum
Lambeth, SE1

1. Date formally established: 1920
2. Architect of present building: James Lewis (1815)
3. Founded by: Act of Parliament
4. Exhibits relate to British and Commonwealth military operations since 1914
5. History: Opened at the Crystal Palace, moved to South Kensington (1924) and then to Lambeth (1936)

London Photographic Atlas: Page 72

Tel: (020) 7416 5000
www.iwm.org.uk

The Imperial War Museum is a relative newcomer to this building, which was completed in 1815 as the central block of the Bethlehem Royal Hospital, better known as the mental hospital, Bedlam, where Charlie Chaplin's mother was among the inmates. The dome and portico on the north front of the building were added in 1835 by Sydney Smirke, who also designed the British Museum's Round Reading Room (p. 10). The two 15-inch guns that can be seen to the north of the museum once saw action on HMS Resolution and HMS Ramillies.

Kew Gardens (Royal Botanic Gardens)
Kew, TW9

1. Date created: 1759 (made public 1840)
2. Laid out by: Princess Augusta, Lord Bute and William Aiton
3. Exhibits: Over 33,000 plant species
4. Area: 300 acres
5. Features: Palm House, Princess of Wales Conservatory, Temperate House, Chinese Pagoda

London Photographic Atlas: Page 153

Tel: (020) 8940 1171
www.rbgkew.org.uk

Kew Gardens began life as a pleasure garden created in 1731 by Prince Frederick, the eldest son of George II. Frederick died in 1751 after being hit by a cricket ball and it was his widow, Princess Augusta (mother of George III), who established the first botanic garden at Kew in 1759. Some of its earliest specimens being brought back from the voyages of Captain Cook, establishing Kew from the start as a centre for botanical research. The original 9-acre garden was later united with the grounds of Richmond Lodge (landscaped by Capability Brown) and, with botanist Sir Joseph Banks as unofficial director, Kew Gardens became famous. The gardens were handed to the nation by Royal Commission in 1840 and a year later Sir William Hooker was appointed the first official director.

Lambeth Palace
Lambeth, SE1

1. Date built: c1200/1828–34
2. Built for: Archbishop Hubert Walter (restored by Edward Blore)
3. Function: Official residence of the Archbishop of Canterbury
4. Features: Tudor gatehouse (1486–1501) built for Archbishop Morton
5. Historic events: Attacked by rioters in 1381 (Wat Tyler), 1640 (London Apprentices) and 1780 (Gordon Riots)

London Photographic Atlas: Page 71

Tel: (020) 7898 1198
www.archbishopofcanterbury.org

Hubert Walter was the first archbishop to live at Lambeth, acquiring the Manor in 1197 and building Lambeth House shortly afterwards. The house was much extended by successive archbishops, and was known as Lambeth Palace by the time Archbishop Matthew Parker died here in 1575. Parker, who is buried in the chapel at Lambeth Palace, was notorious for meddling in state affairs and is thought to be the original "nosey Parker".

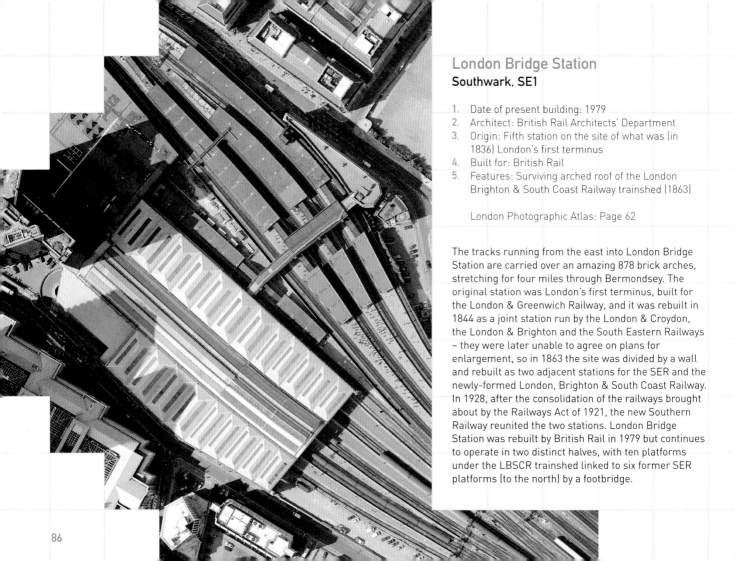

London Bridge Station
Southwark, SE1

1. Date of present building: 1979
2. Architect: British Rail Architects' Department
3. Origin: Fifth station on the site of what was (in 1836) London's first terminus
4. Built for: British Rail
5. Features: Surviving arched roof of the London Brighton & South Coast Railway trainshed (1863)

London Photographic Atlas: Page 62

The tracks running from the east into London Bridge Station are carried over an amazing 878 brick arches, stretching for four miles through Bermondsey. The original station was London's first terminus, built for the London & Greenwich Railway, and it was rebuilt in 1844 as a joint station run by the London & Croydon, the London & Brighton and the South Eastern Railways – they were later unable to agree on plans for enlargement, so in 1863 the site was divided by a wall and rebuilt as two adjacent stations for the SER and the newly-formed London, Brighton & South Coast Railway. In 1928, after the consolidation of the railways brought about by the Railways Act of 1921, the new Southern Railway reunited the two stations. London Bridge Station was rebuilt by British Rail in 1979 but continues to operate in two distinct halves, with ten platforms under the LBSCR trainshed linked to six former SER platforms (to the north) by a footbridge.

London Eye
Lambeth, SE1

1. Date raised: 1999
2. Architects: David Marks and Julia Barfield
3. Diameter (height): 443 ft
4. Weight: 1,900 tonnes
5. Speed: 0.85 ft/sec (30 min per revolution)

London Photographic Atlas: Page 71

Tel: 0870 5000 600
www.ba-londoneye.com

The London Eye is the world's largest observation wheel, revolutionising an idea pioneered in Chicago in 1893 by George Ferris to celebrate the 400th anniversary of the arrival of Columbus in the New World. London's wheel was designed by husband-and-wife team Julia Barfield and David Marks as an entry for a competition organised in 1993 by the Sunday Times and the Architecture Foundation to find ideas for a monument to mark the new millennium. However, the judging panel was not as far-sighted as the organizers, and the prize was not awarded because the judges decided that none of the entries was good enough. Thankfully Barfield and Marks did not give up, and succeeded in creating London's most elegant and exciting millennium landmark.

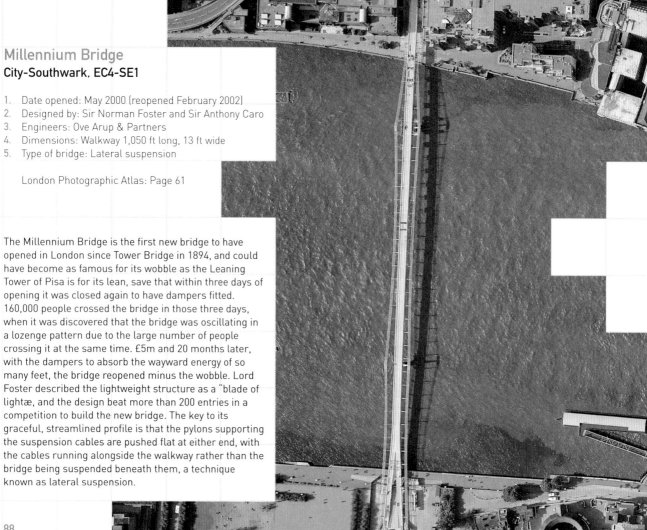

Millennium Bridge
City-Southwark, EC4-SE1

1. Date opened: May 2000 (reopened February 2002)
2. Designed by: Sir Norman Foster and Sir Anthony Caro
3. Engineers: Ove Arup & Partners
4. Dimensions: Walkway 1,050 ft long, 13 ft wide
5. Type of bridge: Lateral suspension

London Photographic Atlas: Page 61

The Millennium Bridge is the first new bridge to have
opened in London since Tower Bridge in 1894, and could
have become as famous for its wobble as the Leaning
Tower of Pisa is for its lean, save that within three days of
opening it was closed again to have dampers fitted.
160,000 people crossed the bridge in those three days,
when it was discovered that the bridge was oscillating in
a lozenge pattern due to the large number of people
crossing it at the same time. £5m and 20 months later,
with the dampers to absorb the wayward energy of so
many feet, the bridge reopened minus the wobble. Lord
Foster described the lightweight structure as a "blade of
lightæ, and the design beat more than 200 entries in a
competition to build the new bridge. The key to its
graceful, streamlined profile is that the pylons supporting
the suspension cables are pushed flat at either end, with
the cables running alongside the walkway rather than the
bridge being suspended beneath them, a technique
known as lateral suspension.

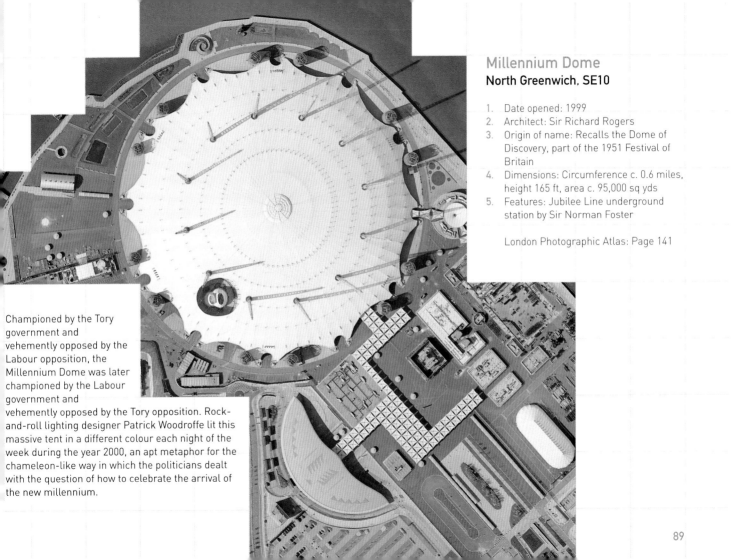

Millennium Dome
North Greenwich, SE10

1. Date opened: 1999
2. Architect: Sir Richard Rogers
3. Origin of name: Recalls the Dome of Discovery, part of the 1951 Festival of Britain
4. Dimensions: Circumference c. 0.6 miles, height 165 ft, area c. 95,000 sq yds
5. Features: Jubilee Line underground station by Sir Norman Foster

London Photographic Atlas: Page 141

Championed by the Tory government and vehemently opposed by the Labour opposition, the Millennium Dome was later championed by the Labour government and vehemently opposed by the Tory opposition. Rock-and-roll lighting designer Patrick Woodroffe lit this massive tent in a different colour each night of the week during the year 2000, an apt metaphor for the chameleon-like way in which the politicians dealt with the question of how to celebrate the arrival of the new millennium.

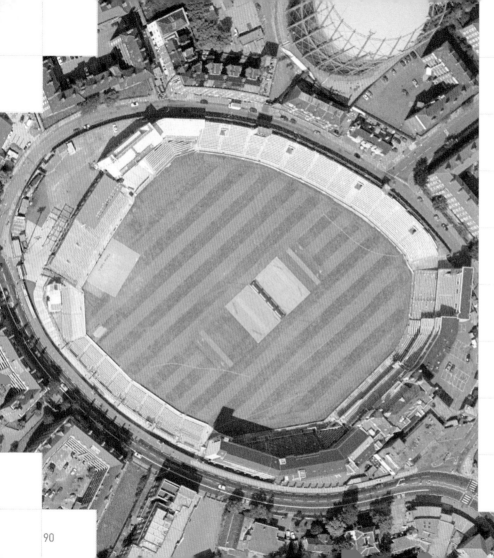

The Oval Cricket Ground
Kennington, SE11

1. Date opened: 1845
2. Built for: Montpelier Cricket Club of Walworth
3. Home club: Surrey County Cricket Club
4. Club founded: 1845
5. Ground capacity: 16,500

London Photographic Atlas: Page 161

Tel: (020) 7582 6660
www.surreyccc.co.uk

The Oval was the venue for the first ever Test match between England and Australia in 1880 and the ground is now firmly associated with cricket, but things might have been different – towards the end of the 19th century CW Alcock, Secretary of the Surrey County Cricket Club, was also the Secretary of the Football Association, and the first ever FA Cup final was played at the Oval in 1872 (Wanderers beat the Royal Engineers 1-0 in front of a crowd of 2,000). Most of the FA Cup finals between 1872 and 1892 were played here, before moving to Crystal Palace (see p. 75) and then to Wembley Stadium (see p. 125).

Peckham Rye Park and Common
Peckham, SE15

1. Date park opened to the public: 1894
2. Date common purchased by Camberwell vestry: 1868
3. Origin of name: Peckham from Anglo-Saxon "village among the hills", Rye thought to be from the crop grown once there
4. Area: Park 49 acres, Common c. 64 acres
5. Historic events: William Blake described seeing a vision of angels in an oak tree here (1765)

London Photographic Atlas: Page 180

The green parkland known as Peckham Rye is in fact two distinct areas, Peckham Rye Common and Peckham Rye Park. The village of Peckham began to be developed in the 19th century after the digging of the Grand Surrey Canal (accelerated by the arrival of the railways) and, in order to prevent the ancient common being built on, the Camberwell vestry bought it in 1868 and made it a public park, though it continued to be known as Peckham Rye Common. The adjacent Homestall Farm was acquired for the public in 1890, and opened as Peckham Rye Park four years later.

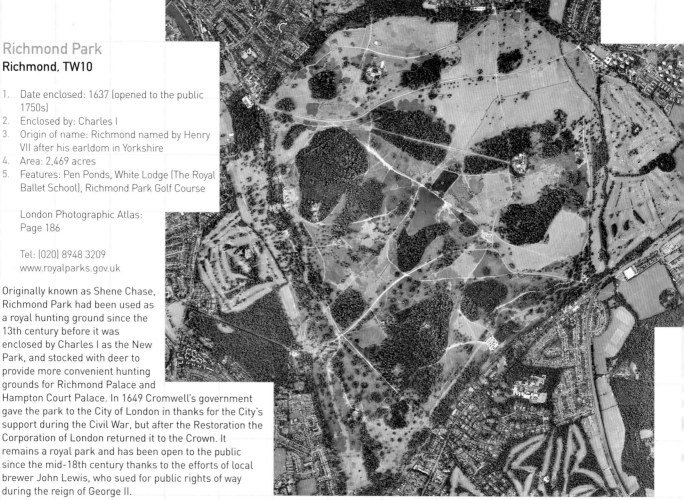

Richmond Park
Richmond, TW10

1. Date enclosed: 1637 (opened to the public 1750s)
2. Enclosed by: Charles I
3. Origin of name: Richmond named by Henry VII after his earldom in Yorkshire
4. Area: 2,469 acres
5. Features: Pen Ponds, White Lodge (The Royal Ballet School), Richmond Park Golf Course

London Photographic Atlas:
Page 186

Tel: (020) 8948 3209
www.royalparks.gov.uk

Originally known as Shene Chase, Richmond Park had been used as a royal hunting ground since the 13th century before it was enclosed by Charles I as the New Park, and stocked with deer to provide more convenient hunting grounds for Richmond Palace and Hampton Court Palace. In 1649 Cromwell's government gave the park to the City of London in thanks for the City's support during the Civil War, but after the Restoration the Corporation of London returned it to the Crown. It remains a royal park and has been open to the public since the mid-18th century thanks to the efforts of local brewer John Lewis, who sued for public rights of way during the reign of George II.

Royal Festival Hall
Lambeth, SE1

1. Date built: 1949-51/1962-65
2. Architect: Sir Robert Matthew and
   JL Martin/Sir Hubert Bennett
3. Origin of name: Built for the 1951 Festival of Britain
4. Features: Uniquely, the auditorium is
   suspended over the open-plan foyer
5. Seating capacity: Varies from 2,299 to 3,111
   according to the type of performance

London Photographic Atlas: Page 59

Tel: (020) 7921 0600
www.rfh.org.uk

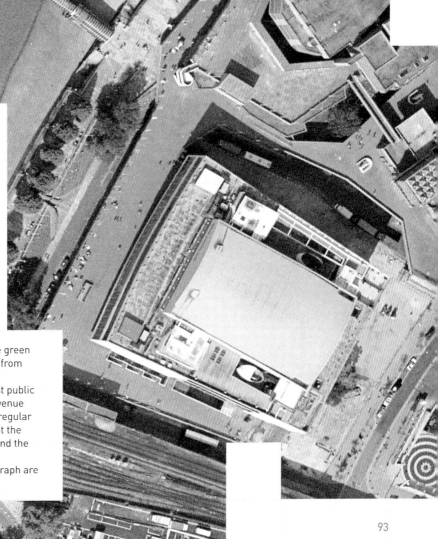

The Royal Festival Hall, easily identifiable by the distinctive green
curved roof of its auditorium, is the only surviving building from
the South Bank Exhibition which was held here in 1951 to
celebrate the centenary of the Great Exhibition and to boost public
morale after the Second World War. The RFH is a popular venue
for choral and orchestral concerts and recitals, and hosts regular
seasons by the English National Ballet. Other attractions at the
1951 South Bank Exhibition included a large ferris wheel and the
Dome of Discovery, themes repeated for the millennium
celebrations half a century later. Also visible in this photograph are
the Queen Elizabeth Hall and Purcell Room (1967) and the
Hayward Gallery (1967).

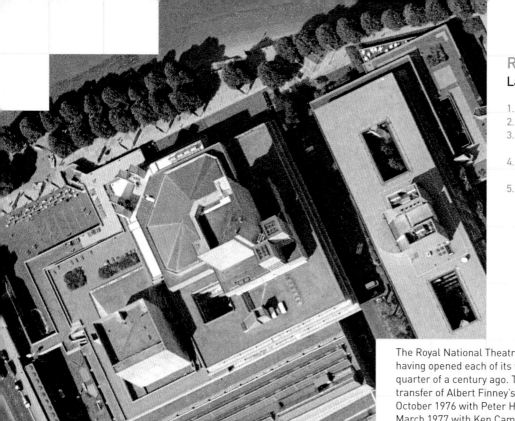

Royal National Theatre
Lambeth, SE1

1. Date built: 1951–77 (opened 1976)
2. Architect: Denys Lasdun
3. National Theatre Company founded: 1962 (based at the Old Vic until 1976/77)
4. Features: 3 theatres – the Lyttelton, the Olivier and the Cottesloe
5. Seating capacity: Olivier c. 1,150/Lyttelton c. 890/Cottesloe c. 300 (all vary according to circumstances)

London Photographic Atlas: Page 59

Tel: (020) 7452 3400
www.nationaltheatre.org.uk

The Royal National Theatre celebrated its 25th anniversary in 2001, having opened each of its three theatres as they were completed a quarter of a century ago. The Lyttelton opened in March 1976 with a transfer of Albert Finney's Hamlet, the Olivier seven months later in October 1976 with Peter Hall's Tamburlaine, and the Cottesloe in March 1977 with Ken Campbell's Illuminatus. The idea of a national theatre was first mooted in 1848 but it was to be over a century later before the National Theatre Bill was eventually passed in 1949. Princess Elizabeth (now HM The Queen) laid the foundation stone for the new building in 1951, the theatre company itself was founded in 1962, and it was 1976 before the company was finally able to move into its new home.

Royal Naval College and Queen's House
Greenwich, SE10

1. Date built: 1664–1742 (RNC)/1616–38 (QH)
2. Architect: Sir Christopher Wren (RNC)/Inigo Jones (QH)
3. Origin: Built on the site of Greenwich Palace (RNC)/Completed for Queen Henrietta Maria, wife of Charles I (QH)
4. Functions: Hospital for disabled seamen, RN college, University of Greenwich (RNC)/Crown property, Royal Naval Asylum, National Maritime Museum (QH)
5. Historic events: Lord Nelson lay in state here before the funeral procession made its way by boat to St Paul's (RNC)

London Photographic Atlas: Page 167

The four buildings to the north of the picture are still known as the Royal Naval College, although they are now part of the University of Greenwich. They were built as a naval hospital corresponding to the army's Chelsea Hospital (p. 33), and after the demise of the hospital in 1869, the RNC occupied the buildings until 1997. Queen's House was originally an H-shaped building straddling what was then the Deptford-Woolwich road, the north and south wings being linked by a bridge. In 1662 John Webb added two first floor rooms, closing the sides of the "H" and creating the square plan seen here.

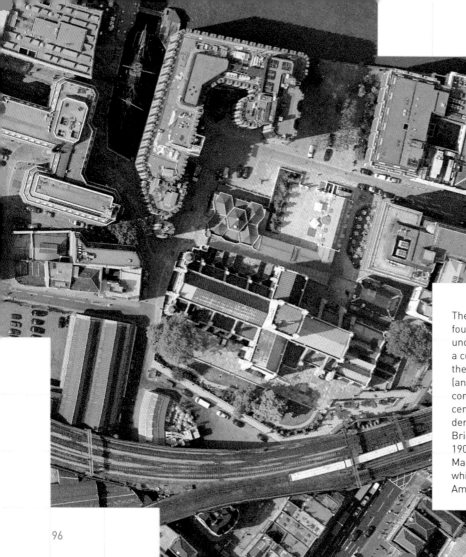

Southwark Cathedral
Southwark, SE1

1. Date built: c. 1213–1520
2. Architect: Richard Mason
3. Dedicated to: St Saviour and St Mary Overie
4. Height of tower: 163 ft
5. Denomination: Church of England

London Photographic Atlas: Page 62

Tel: (020) 7367 6700
www.dswark.org

The very thing that provided the means for the foundation of Southwark Cathedral was almost its undoing – a Thames river crossing. Tradition has it that a convent was founded here in the 7th century and that the nuns obtained revenue from a ferry across the river (another version of the story is that the church and convent were built by a ferryman), but during the 19th century the chapel at the east end of the church was demolished to make way for John Rennie's new London Bridge. The church, which attained cathedral status in 1905, contains a monument to the victims of the Marchioness disaster, and also the Harvard Chapel, which commemorates John Harvard, founder of the American university, who was baptised here.

Surrey Quays Shopping Centre
Rotherhithe, SE16

1. Date opened: 1988
2. Architects: Fitzroy Robinson
3. Origin of name: Built on the site of Surrey Commercial Docks ('The Surreys')
4. Area: c. 24 acres
5. History: Originally developed by Tesco, now owned by Shopping Centres Ltd (Tesco & Slough Estates)

London Photographic Atlas: Page 149

Tel: (020) 7237 5282
www.surreyquaysshoppingcentre.co.uk

At their height the Surrey Commercial Docks included nine separate docks and six timber ponds, the main trade being softwood from Scandinavia, Canada and the Baltic – a past that is recalled in the names given to parts of the new development, such as Deal Porter's Way, Timber Pond Road, Finland Street and Canada Water (the body of water seen to the north of the shopping centre). The docks were closed in 1970, filled, and sold off during the 1980s. Surrey Quays Shopping Centre was originally developed by Tesco with the encouragement of the London Docklands Development Corporation, and is now home to over 50 retailers.

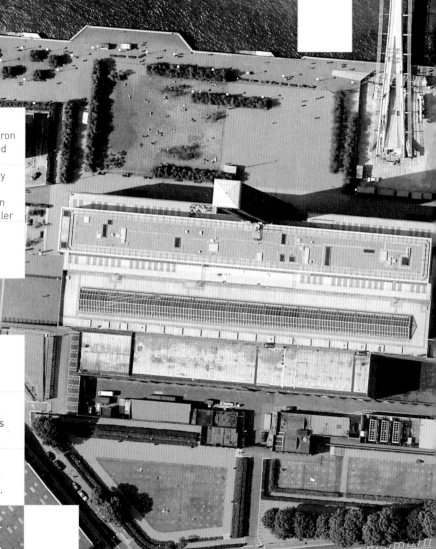

Tate Modern (formerly Bankside Power Station)

Bankside, SE1

1. Date opened: 1963/2000
2. Architects: Sir Giles Gilbert Scott/Herzog & de Meuron
3. Origin of name: Offshoot of the Tate Gallery, founded by sugar magnate Sir Henry Tate
4. Exhibits: Modern art collection from the Tate Gallery (now Tate Britain) at Millbank
5. Features: Planning permission for the power station stipulated that the single chimney should not be taller than St Paul's

London Photographic Atlas: Page 61

Tel: (020) 7401 5000
www.tate.org.uk

Bankside Power Station was designed by Sir Giles Gilbert Scott, the architect of Battersea Power Station, and operated from 1963 until 1980. The origins of the Tate Gallery are much older, opening in 1897 as the National Gallery of British Art using money donated by Sir Henry Tate, who also gave his collection of paintings and sculptures. At the turn of the 21st century, Scott's massive power station was transformed into a gallery to house the Tate's collection of modern art. The new gallery opened in 2000 as Tate Modern, after which the Tate Gallery on Millbank was rebranded as Tate Britain.

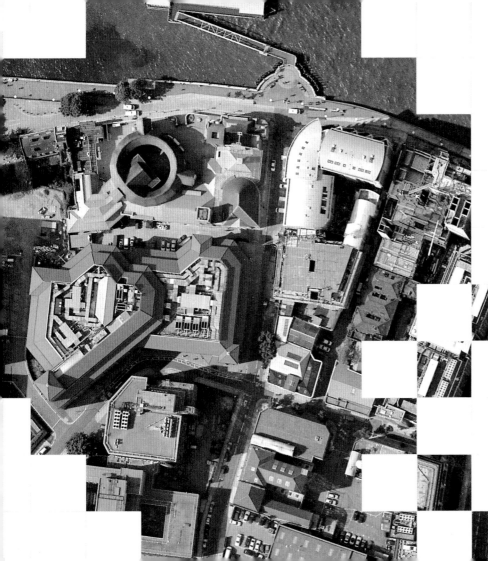

Shakespeare's Globe
Bankside, SE1

1. Date opened: 1997
2. Founded by: Sam Wanamaker
3. Origin of name: Reconstruction of the original Globe Theatre (1599)
4. Features: The first thatched roof in London since the Great Fire
5. Historic events: Opened by HM The Queen (1997)

London Photographic Atlas: Page 61

Tel: (020) 7902 1500
www.shakespeares-globe.org

In his prologue to King Henry V, Shakespeare asks "may we cram within this wooden 'O' the very casques that did affright the air at Agincourt?" and seen from the air it is easy to understand why he described his theatre as a wooden 'O'. This reconstruction, close to the site of the original Globe Theatre, is the realization of a dream long-held by the late American actor and director Sam Wanamaker.

Waterloo Station and Waterloo International Station
Lambeth, SE1

1. Date of present building: 1921/1993
2. Architects: JR Scott/Nicholas Grimshaw & Partners
3. Origin of name: Commemorates Wellington's victory at the Battle of Waterloo
4. Built for: London & South Western Railway/Eurostar
5. Features: British Rail's war memorial the Victory Arch. The international platforms are among the longest in the world

London Photographic Atlas: Page 71

The original Waterloo Station was built in 1848 for the London & South Western Railway, and it gradually expanded until its haphazard conglomeration of platforms, including two sets both numbered 1 and 2, made it "the most perplexing railway station in London". It was rebuilt from 1900-21 with its distinctive ridge-and-furrow roof, 21 platforms and a massive 120 ft by 770 ft concourse. Four platforms on the western edge of the station were demolished in 1990 to make way for the international station which now shelters under the steel and glass panels of Nicholas Grimshaw's curved roof.

Wetland Centre
Barn Elms, SW13

1. Date opened: 26th May 2000
2. Laid out by: Wetland Advisory Agency
3. Origin: Built on the site of the Barn
   Elms Reservoirs
4. Area: 105 acres
5. History: The Wildfowl & Wetlands Trust
   was founded by Sir Peter Scott in 1946

London Photographic Atlas: Page 156

Tel: (020) 8409 4400
www.wetlandcentre.org.uk

The Wetland Centre was created from
1995–2000 as a sanctuary for wetland birds
whose natural habitat is fast disappearing.
The Barn Elms Reservoirs, already
designated a Site of Special Scientific
Interest, became redundant after the
building of Thames Water's London Tunnel
Ring Main (a 50-mile tunnel 130 feet below
ground) and the Wildfowl and Wetlands
Trust stepped in to transform the concrete
reservoirs into an urban wetland reserve.
Sir David Attenborough described the
resulting Wetland Centre as "an ideal
model for how the natural world and
humanity might exist alongside one another
in the centuries to come."

Wimbledon (All England Lawn Tennis & Croquet Club)
Wimbledon, SW19

1. Date opened: 1922 (redeveloped 1994-c. 2004)
2. Architects: Try Construction (Centre Court); BDP (No1 Court)
3. Home club: The All England Lawn Tennis and Croquet Club
4. Club Founded: 1868 as The All England Croquet Club
5. Stadium capacity: Centre Court 13,813 seated; No. 1 Court 11,429 seated; No2 Court 2,220 seated and 770 standing

London Photographic Atlas: Page 189

Tel: (020) 8946 6131
www.wimbledon.org

But for the audacity of a croquet club, Lord's could have been the home of tennis instead of Wimbledon. The first rules for tennis were drawn up by the MCC at Lord's in 1875, based on a game introduced by Major Walter Clopton Wingfield, who called it "sphairistike" – not surprisingly, the name didn't stick. Two years later, the All England Croquet Club changed its name to the All England Croquet and Lawn Tennis Club and instituted the first Lawn Tennis Championship. New rules were drawn up, and the game has been administered by the All England Club ever since. In 1922 the club moved to the present ground, where 27,000 kilos of strawberries and 7,000 litres of cream are now consumed each year during Championships Fortnight.

north and west

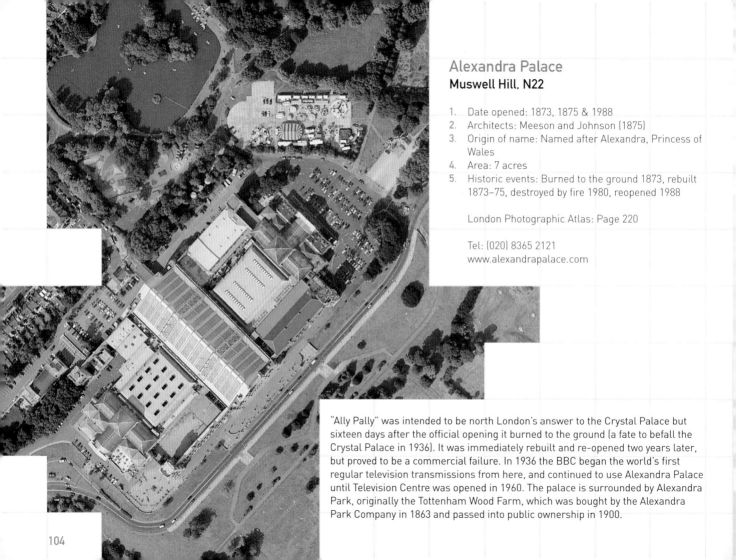

Alexandra Palace
Muswell Hill, N22

1. Date opened: 1873, 1875 & 1988
2. Architects: Meeson and Johnson (1875)
3. Origin of name: Named after Alexandra, Princess of Wales
4. Area: 7 acres
5. Historic events: Burned to the ground 1873, rebuilt 1873–75, destroyed by fire 1980, reopened 1988

London Photographic Atlas: Page 220

Tel: (020) 8365 2121
www.alexandrapalace.com

"Ally Pally" was intended to be north London's answer to the Crystal Palace but sixteen days after the official opening it burned to the ground (a fate to befall the Crystal Palace in 1936). It was immediately rebuilt and re-opened two years later, but proved to be a commercial failure. In 1936 the BBC began the world's first regular television transmissions from here, and continued to use Alexandra Palace until Television Centre was opened in 1960. The palace is surrounded by Alexandra Park, originally the Tottenham Wood Farm, which was bought by the Alexandra Park Company in 1863 and passed into public ownership in 1900.

BBC Television Centre
Shepherd's Bush, W12

1. Date built: 1951–60/1985–98
2. Architect: Graham Dawbarn (new development by John Mowlem plc)
3. Origin: Part of the White City site of the 1908 Franco-British Exhibition
4. Area: 13.5 acres
5. Features: 40 ft obelisk with bronze figure of Helios (TB Huxley), "Reclining Figure – Hand" (Henry Moore)

London Photographic Atlas: Page 136

Tel: 0870 6030304
www.bbc.co.uk

Television Centre was the world's first purpose-built television broadcasting centre, and was described as "a factory for the production of electronic programmes" when it opened in 1960. The Centre's unique design, quite clear from the air, is based on a question mark doodled on an envelope by architect Graham Dawbarn as he pondered on the challenge of designing the home of public service television production. The East Tower was added during the 1960s, beginning a march of construction eastwards that was completed in 1998 with the News Centre and main reception fronting onto Wood Lane, making the entire Centre look more like Dawbarn's question mark than it did when it was first completed.

Brent Reservoir
(Welsh Harp Reservoir)
West Hendon/Neasden, NW9 & NW2

1. Date dammed: 1834-35
2. Built for: Regent's Canal Company (later the Grand Union Canal)
3. Origin of name: Named after a former alehouse on the Edgware Road
4. Features: Sailing centre, Cool Oak Bridge
5. Historic events: The first mechanical hare was used in a greyhound race here (1876)

London Photographic Atlas: Page 93

The Welsh Harp Reservoir was created when the River Brent was dammed in order to give greater pressure to the canal feeder through Stonebridge, which is where the River Brent meets the Grand Union Canal. The reservoir and the Welsh Harp pub after which it is named became such popular places of entertainment at the end of the 19th century that they are referred to in several Victorian music-hall songs.

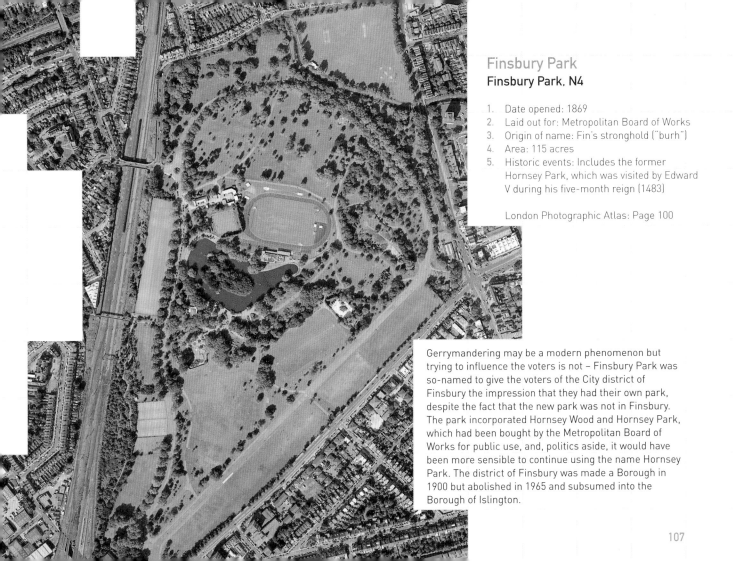

Finsbury Park
Finsbury Park, N4

1. Date opened: 1869
2. Laid out for: Metropolitan Board of Works
3. Origin of name: Fin's stronghold ("burh")
4. Area: 115 acres
5. Historic events: Includes the former Hornsey Park, which was visited by Edward V during his five-month reign (1483)

London Photographic Atlas: Page 100

Gerrymandering may be a modern phenomenon but trying to influence the voters is not – Finsbury Park was so-named to give the voters of the City district of Finsbury the impression that they had their own park, despite the fact that the new park was not in Finsbury. The park incorporated Hornsey Wood and Hornsey Park, which had been bought by the Metropolitan Board of Works for public use, and, politics aside, it would have been more sensible to continue using the name Hornsey Park. The district of Finsbury was made a Borough in 1900 but abolished in 1965 and subsumed into the Borough of Islington.

Hampstead Heath
Hampstead, NW3

1. Date springs discovered: 1698
2. Foiled developer: Sir Thomas Maryon Wilson
3. Origin: Became popular after the discovery of medicinal springs
4. Area: 791 acres, including Parliament Hill (271 acres) and Golders Hill (36 acres)
5. Features: Parliament Hill (319 ft), Kenwood, Jack Straw's Castle

London Photographic Atlas: Page 97

Hampstead owes its initial attraction to the discovery in 1698 of chalybeate springs said to be "of the same nature and equal in virtue with Tunbridge Wells". The Heath itself is fortunate to have survived the 19th century – between 1831 and 1871, Lord of the Manor Sir Thomas Maryon-Wilson introduced fifteen Parliamentary Bills in an attempt to win permission to build on it.

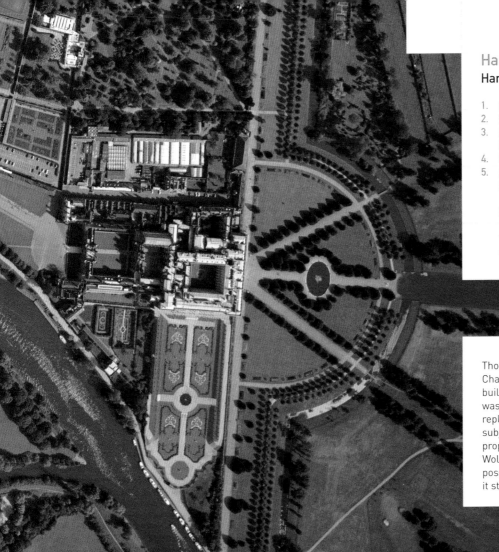

Hampton Court Palace
Hampton Court, KT8

1. Date built: c. 1514-40/1689-1727
2. Remodelled by: Sir Christopher Wren
3. Origin of name: Hampton from the Saxon "farm on the bend in the river"
4. Family connection: Wolsey/Crown
5. Historic events: Birth of the future Edward VI (1537)

London Photographic Atlas: Page 267

Tel: (020) 8781 9500
www.hrp.org.uk

Thomas Wolsey, Cardinal and Lord Chancellor, built at Hampton Court a building of such splendour that Henry VIII was prompted to ask why. Wolsey reputedly replied, "To show how noble a place a subject may offer his sovereign" – prophetic words indeed, because when Wolsey fell from favour Henry took possession of Hampton Court and extended it still further for his own use.

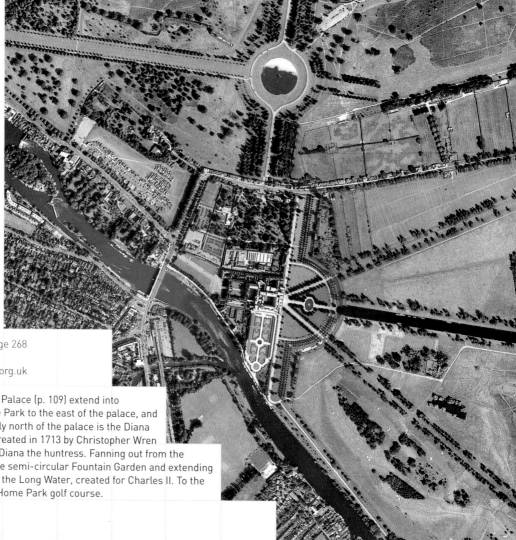

Hampton Court Park and Bushy Park

Hampton Court, KT8 & TW11

1. Date laid out: 16th–18th century
2. Laid out for: Henry VIII, Charles II, William & Mary
3. Origin: Both parks once belonged to the Knights Hospitallers of St John, were acquired by Cardinal Wolsey and passed with Hampton Court Palace to Henry VIII
4. Area: 622 acres (HCP)/1,099 acres (BP)
5. Features: Broad Walk (Henry VIII), Long Water (Charles II), Fountain Garden and Diana Fountain (William & Mary)

London Photographic Atlas: Page 268

Tel: (020) 8781 9500   www.hrp.org.uk

The grounds of Hampton Court Palace (p. 109) extend into Hampton Court Park and Home Park to the east of the palace, and Bushy Park to the north. Directly north of the palace is the Diana Fountain in its circular basin, created in 1713 by Christopher Wren and surmounted by a statue of Diana the huntress. Fanning out from the eastern front of the palace is the semi-circular Fountain Garden and extending out from the central pathway is the Long Water, created for Charles II. To the south of the Long Water is the Home Park golf course.

Hanger Lane Gyratory
Park Royal, W5

1. Date built: 1980
2. Built by: Department of Transport
3. Purpose: Intersection of A40 Western Avenue with A406 North Circular and A4005 Hanger Lane
4. Peak traffic flow: 8,000 vehicles per hour
5. Features: Amoco House, Hanger Lane Underground station

London Photographic Atlas: Page 123

The word gyratory entered motoring parlance in 1980 when the crossroads at Hanger Lane was transformed into a roundabout that is not a roundabout. A new name was needed, and it is a name all too familiar to anyone who has ever listened to the traffic news, because the Hanger Lane Gyratory, built to ease traffic congestion, is congested with traffic every morning and every evening. This huge rectangle of concrete and tarmac works like a roundabout, although it is the wrong shape, with eight lanes of traffic on the eastern side, slip roads leading every which way, the overground Tube line passing underneath (the station is at the south-eastern corner) and a tunnel under its southern edge for through traffic on the A40.

Heathrow Airport
Harmondsworth, TW6

1. Date opened: 1929 (reopened as a civil airport 1946)
2. Operated by: British Airports Authority (BAA)
3. Air transport movements (2000): 460,476
4. Passengers (2000): 64,620,286
5. Runways: 09R/27L 12,000ft; 09L/27R 12,802ft; 05/23 6,450ft

London Photographic Atlas: Page 256

Tel: 0870 000 0123
www.heathrow.com

When the first aerodrome was built at Heathrow by Richard Fairey in 1929, on land bought from the vicar of Harmondsworth, local residents were placated by the fact that it was a test site and therefore there would be very few flights! During the Second World War the Air Ministry decided to develop Heathrow with the long term view of using it as a civil airport after the war, and used emergency wartime powers for the compulsory purchase of land which included Fairey's aerodrome. The civilian airport opened in 1946, and just over half a century later Heathrow is the world's busiest passenger airport and second biggest cargo airport, with plans for a fifth terminal handling an extra 30 million passengers every year.

Highbury Stadium
Highbury, N5

1. Date opened: 1913
2. Built for: Henry Norris
3. Home club: Arsenal Football Club
4. Club founded: 1886
5. Stadium capacity: 38,500

London Photographic Atlas: Page 100

Tel: (020) 7704 4000
www.arsenal.com

Just as Chelsea do not play in Chelsea and Millwall do not play in Millwall, so Arsenal do not play anywhere near the Arsenal. Taking their name from the Royal Arsenal at Woolwich, the Gunners moved north of the river in 1913, three years after Millwall had moved in the opposite direction. Property developer Henry Norris took control of Arsenal in 1910 and, following their relegation shortly afterwards, he decided that a change of home might mean a change of fortune. He took out a lease on the sports ground of St John's College of Divinity and there built the first Highbury Stadium, where the inaugural game was played on 6th September 1913, against Leicester. At one time crowds of up to 70,000 watched Arsenal (and England) play at Highbury, but with new safety regulations and the advent of all-seater stadia, the capacity of Highbury has been reduced to just over half that figure.

Hogarth Roundabout
Chiswick, W4

1. Date built: 1925–1960s (Great West Road built)
2. Built for: Department of Transport
3. Origin of name: Stands close to Hogarth's House, country home of the artist William Hogarth
4. Purpose: Intersection of A4 Great West Road with A316 and other minor roads
5. Features: Hogarth's House, Fuller's Brewery, single-lane flyover

London Photographic Atlas: Page 155

Tel: Hogarth's House (020) 8994 6757

A name infamous to anyone who listens to the traffic news, the Hogarth Roundabout is characterised by the frail-looking single-lane flyover that carries through traffic on the A316 over the roundabout on its spindly steel legs. 50 yards to the west is Hogarth's House, the country retreat where William Hogarth and his family came to find peace and quiet each summer from 1749 until 1764. To the east is Fuller, Smith and Turner's Griffin Brewery, continuing a tradition of brewing on this site that dates back to the time of Elizabeth I, and now home of the famous Fuller's London Pride.

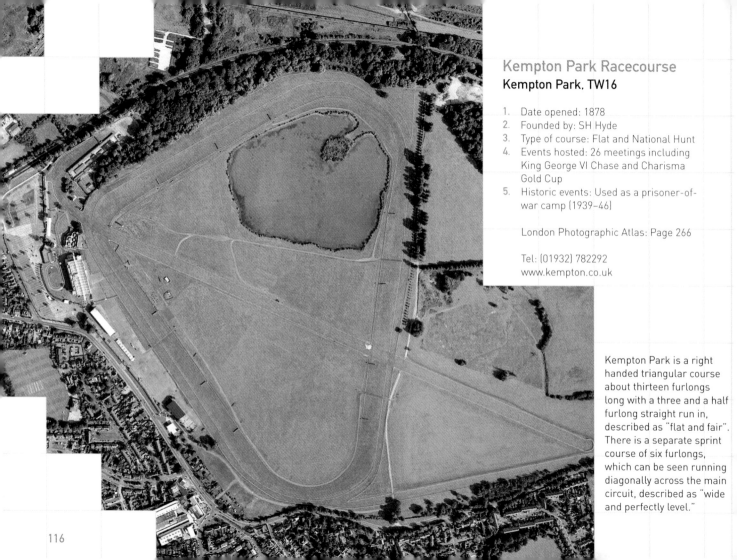

Kempton Park Racecourse
Kempton Park, TW16

1. Date opened: 1878
2. Founded by: SH Hyde
3. Type of course: Flat and National Hunt
4. Events hosted: 26 meetings including King George VI Chase and Charisma Gold Cup
5. Historic events: Used as a prisoner-of-war camp (1939–46)

London Photographic Atlas: Page 266

Tel: (01932) 782292
www.kempton.co.uk

Kempton Park is a right handed triangular course about thirteen furlongs long with a three and a half furlong straight run in, described as "flat and fair". There is a separate sprint course of six furlongs, which can be seen running diagonally across the main circuit, described as "wide and perfectly level."

Kenwood
Hampstead, NW3

1. Date built: c. 1616/1764–79
2. Remodelled by: Robert Adam
3. Origin of name: Uncertain – possibly from Caen Wood
4. Family connection: Brydges/Bute/Mansfield/Iveagh
5. Historic events: Lord Iveagh, head of the Guinness family, bequeathed the house, contents and grounds to the nation (1927)

London Photographic Atlas: Page 97

Tel: (020) 8348 1286
www.english-heritage.org.uk

It is by two strokes of luck that Kenwood House has survived for public view. Not only was it saved for the nation from developers by Lord Iveagh but it was almost ransacked by the Gordon rioters in 1780. The 1st Earl of Mansfield, then owner of the house, was a deeply unpopular Attorney-General and Lord Chief Justice, having sent 102 people to the gallows and sentenced a further 448 to transportation. The rioters had already ransacked his Bloomsbury house and were making their way towards Kenwood when they were distracted en route by the landlord of the Spaniards Inn, who happened to be an ex-butler of Mansfield's – he gave the rioters free drinks until soldiers arrived to disarm the now-drunken mob, whose muskets can still be seen in the saloon bar of the pub.

Lord's Cricket Ground
St John's Wood, NW8

1. Date moved to present site: 1814
2. Laid out for: Thomas Lord
3. Home club: Marylebone Cricket Club (MCC)
4. Club founded: 1787
5. Ground capacity: 29,500

London Photographic Atlas: Page 30

Tel: (020) 7432 1033
www.lords.org

Lord's is the world's most famous cricket ground and the home of the Ashes, the MCC and a stuffed sparrow that was "bowled out" by Jehangir Khan in 1936. Yorkshireman Thomas Lord set up his first ground in Marylebone in 1787, but an increase in rent forced him to move to North Bank, St John's Wood. Three years later he had to move to the present site when the MCC discovered that the Regent's Canal was to cut across the playing area. Eighty-five years after that it was a railway that was to cut across the playing area, but this time the MCC won the battle – the club acquired extra land in exchange for allowing the railway company to tunnel under the practice pitch to reach Marylebone Station.

M25/M4 Interchange
Iver, Berkshire

1. Date built: c. 1980–84
2. Built by: Department of Transport
3. Junction number: M25 jct15, M4 jct4b
4. Peak traffic flow: 180,000 vehicles per hour
5. Features: Almost perfect clover-leaf intersection

London Photographic Atlas: Page 248

There is a saying that all roads in England lead to London and all roads in London lead to the centre but, like most sayings, it is not quite true – the M25 just goes round in a large, slightly distorted circle. This junction is where London's orbital motorway meets one of the major radials and the view from the air makes perfect sense of the tangle of sliproads that appears so confusing at ground level. The M25 forms just 6% of Britain's motorway network but carries 14% of motorway traffic. Part of its purpose is to keep lorries and long-distance traffic out of London, making it the world's longest bypass, but the frequent queues of stationary vehicles have led to it also being dubbed the world's most expensive car park.

Osterley Park
Osterley, TW7

1. Date built: 1575/1761–80
2. Remodelled by: Robert Adam
3. Origin of name: Sheep-fold meadow or grove ("eowestre", sheep-fold, and "lea", meadow, or "leah", gove)
4. Family connection: Gresham/Child/Earls of Jersey
5. Features: 140 hectares of park and farmland

London Photographic Atlas: Page 251

Tel: (020) 8232 5050
www.osterleypark.org.uk

The first mansion at Osterley Park was built for Sir Thomas Gresham, founder of the Royal Exchange, and it was later rebuilt by Robert Adam for another City merchant, Francis Child, the founder of Child's Bank. Osterley Park might never have become open to public view were it not for the fact that Sarah Anne Child eloped to Gretna Green with the Earl of Westmoreland in 1782 and thereby lost her inheritance. The Child fortune, including Osterley Park, went instead to her younger sister Sophia, who married the Earl of Jersey in 1804 – their descendant the 9th Earl gave the property to the National Trust in 1949.

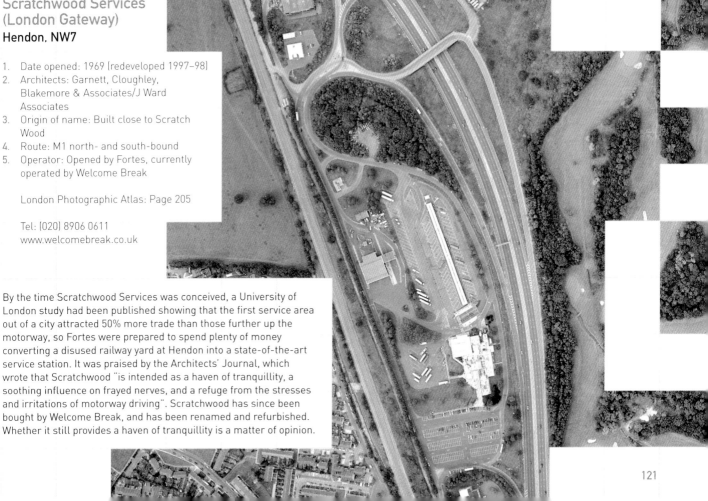

Scratchwood Services (London Gateway)
Hendon, NW7

1. Date opened: 1969 (redeveloped 1997–98)
2. Architects: Garnett, Cloughley, Blakemore & Associates/J Ward Associates
3. Origin of name: Built close to Scratch Wood
4. Route: M1 north- and south-bound
5. Operator: Opened by Fortes, currently operated by Welcome Break

London Photographic Atlas: Page 205

Tel: (020) 8906 0611
www.welcomebreak.co.uk

By the time Scratchwood Services was conceived, a University of London study had been published showing that the first service area out of a city attracted 50% more trade than those further up the motorway, so Fortes were prepared to spend plenty of money converting a disused railway yard at Hendon into a state-of-the-art service station. It was praised by the Architects' Journal, which wrote that Scratchwood "is intended as a haven of tranquillity, a soothing influence on frayed nerves, and a refuge from the stresses and irritations of motorway driving". Scratchwood has since been bought by Welcome Break, and has been renamed and refurbished. Whether it still provides a haven of tranquillity is a matter of opinion.

Shepperton Studios
Shepperton, TW17

1. Date opened: 1932, as Sound City
2. Built for: Norman Loudon
3. Origin: Arranged around Littleton Park House (built 1689 for Thomas Wood)
4. First feature films: "Reunion" and "Watch Beverley" (1932); first TV "The Third Man" (1959)
5. Features: The ghost of a spurned lover who threw herself from the Minstrel's Gallery of Littleton House

London Photographic Atlas: Page 280

Tel: (01932) 562611
www.sheppertonstudios.co.uk

Shepperton Studios is part of a legendary triumvirate of British studios, along with Pinewood and Elstree, but whereas the other two were historically owned and run by companies producing, distributing and exhibiting their own films, Shepperton has always been independent. Shepperton has a reputation within the industry for being a friendly studio, a reputation borne out by Dirk Bogarde's reminiscence: "Shepperton was my favourite studio. I loved all the nonsense of [Littleton] House and the big black and white tiled floor which we had to cross to get to the restaurant and bar.... I remember the story of the dotty lady who threw herself from the gallery into the hall and died, naturally enough. A lot of actors rather wished that they could follow her course having been to rushes."

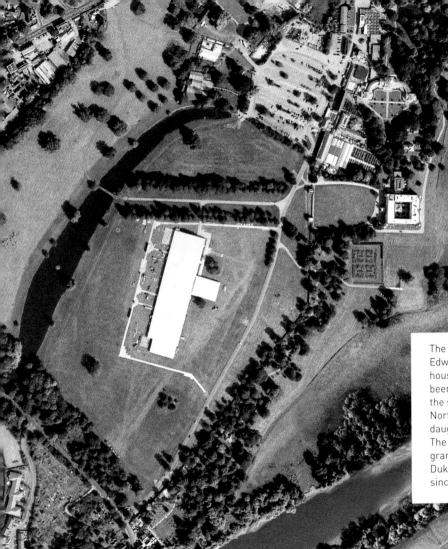

Syon House and Park
Isleworth, TW8

1. Date built: 16th/17th/18th centuries
2. Remodelled by: Inigo Jones (17th century)/Robert Adam (18th century)
3. Park laid out by: Capability Brown (18th century, opened to the public 1837)
4. Family connection: Duke of Somerset/Duke of Northumberland/Crown/Dukes of Northumberland Features: Great Conservatory (Charles
5. Fowler), Garden Centre (Britain's first in 1965), London Butterfly House, London Aquatic Experience

London Photographic Atlas: Page 152

Tel: (020) 8560 0881
www.syonpark.co.uk

The first two owners of Syon House were both executed. Edward Seymour, Duke of Somerset, who built the house on the site of a Brigittine monastery that had been annexed by Henry VIII, was executed for felony and the subsequent owner John Dudley, Duke of Northumberland, for offering the crown to his daughter-in-law Lady Jane Grey, the "nine days queen". The property then reverted to the Crown and was later granted by Elizabeth I to the Percys, Earls and later Dukes of Northumberland, whose home it has been since 1594.

Twickenham Stadium
Twickenham, TW1

1. Date opened: 1909 (redevelopment completed 1995)
2. Built for: The Rugby Football Union
3. Origin of name: Disputed – either "land at the river fork" or "Twicca's riverside land"
4. Stadium capacity: 74,000
5. Historic events: The first Rugby League team to play here was Wigan, when they won the 1996 Twickenham Sevens

London Photographic Atlas: Page 259

Tel: (020) 8892 2000   www.rfu.com

As rugby union's national stadium, Twickenham is owned not by one particular club but by the sport's governing body, the Rugby Football Union. In 1863 several football clubs outlawed the handling of the ball (among other things) and formed the Football Association – eight years later, in 1871, the clubs that had decided to stay with the handling game met at the Pall Mall Restaurant and formed the RFU: rugby and soccer (a corruption of "association") were divided forever. The RFU acquired its own stadium in 1909 when William Williams bought a 10.25 acre site that became known as "Billy Williams's Cabbage Patch". Stands and terracing were built to accommodate 13,000 spectators, and the Twickenham stadium has been expanding ever since, with a further 7 acres of land added to the site in 1921, and major redevelopments in 1921, 1931, 1981, 1990 and 1995.

Wembley Stadium
Wembley, HA9

1. Date built: 1922–23 as the Empire Stadium
2. Architects: Sir John Simpson and Maxwell Ayrton
3. Origin: Built for the British Empire Exhibition of 1924–25
4. Stadium capacity: c. 80,000
5. Events hosted: 1948 Olympic Games, 1966 Soccer World Cup, Live Aid (1982), 1995 Rugby League World Cup, Euro '96

London Photographic Atlas: Page 108

Tel: (020) 8902 8833
www.wembleynationalstadium.com

A close look reveals that a match was taking place at the time this photograph was taken, with packed stands and a packed coach park. The Empire Stadium was completed in time for the 1923 FA Cup final, in which Bolton Wanderers beat West Ham, after which Wembley took over from Crystal Palace as the traditional home of the cup final. England won soccer's World Cup here in 1966 and the "venue of legends" has been considered the spiritual home of English football ever since. In April 1996 Foster & Partners drew up plans to redevelop the stadium and the surrounding area into a new National Stadium but six years later the plans have still not been realized.

White Hart Lane Stadium
Tottenham, N17

1. Date opened: 1899 (redeveloped 1980–98)
2. Architect: Archibald Leitch/Club architect Igal Yawpez
3. Home club: Tottenham Hotspur Football Club
4. Club founded: 1882
5. Stadium capacity: 36,211

London Photographic Atlas: Page 222

Tel: (020) 8365 5000
www.spurs.co.uk

The White Hart Lane stadium (which is not actually on White Hart Lane) stands on land previously owned by the Charrington brewery, where the landlord of the White Hart pub had taken advantage of the fertile soil to set up a nursery. Spurs rented the land in 1899 and set up temporary stands: by 1904 there was a small covered main stand, and the club bought the freehold the following year, but it wasn't until 1909, having secured Football League status, that Archibald Leitch was called in to build the first substantial stadium – and by the end of that season the famous cockerel was adorning the new stand. White Hart Lane has seen many improvements and expansions since, and has recently undergone another massive redevelopment.

Wormwood Scrubs Prison
Wormwood Scrubs, W12

1. Date built: 1874–90
2. Architect: Sir Edmund Du Cane
3. Origin of name: Originally "snake-infested wood", with the later addition of Scrubs, meaning scrubland
4. Inmates: Certified accommodation for 1,050
5. Historic events: The spy George Blake escaped (1966), riots in protest at conditions (1979)

London Photographic Atlas: Page 136

HM Prison Wormwood Scrubs was built almost entirely by prisoners. Contractors built a small, temporary prison to house nine prisoners who built the first block, housing fifty prisoners who then accelerated the building of the second block, allowing one hundred to work on the third, and so on. The prison was designed on a new principle of separate blocks to solve the problems of ventilation and light inherent in the earlier radial system, and each of the four parallel blocks initially worked as a self-contained prison, though they have since been linked by the addition of further blocks to the north of the site. The prison, Britain's largest, is undergoing further development in this photograph.

Index